Contents

Cover photo:
@jasminsleeman

Spiritual Development

50 Bringing Awareness to Now
    By Emily Filmore

60 Finding Peace Inside & Out
    By Sarah Cody

Physical Development

10 Toxic Toys
    By Dr. Sarah Lantz

17 Springtime Allergies
    By Nareen Bizzell

49 It's the Lonely Fruit that get Spoiled
    By Melanie Wright

52 Give your kids the best Start in Life
    ~ Go Organic
    By Lisa Guy

56 Baby Led Weaning
    By Tracey Murkett

Mum and Dad's Development

22 Fatherhood: Joys & Challenges
    in the Early Days
    By Darren Mattock

26 Placenta Encapsulation:
    Revival of an Ancient
    Medical Tradition
    By Kristin Bechedahl

63 Avoiding Mastitis
    By Kate Hale

Emotional Development

8   5 Ways to Encourage (Rather than Praise)
    By Kelly Bartlett

15 Conscious Parenting:
    What's & Why's
    By Prue Blackmore

18 Can You Hear Me Now?
    By Bonnie Harris

20 Gender: Do Differences Really Exist?
    By Claire Eaton

36 Tantrums: Evaporate or Nurture?
    By Naomi Aldot

40 Children & Trauma: What Helps?
    By Petrea King

43 Music for Bonding
    By Tara Hashambhoy

44 Handling Aggression: Part 1
    By Rachel Schofield

64 Nurturing Freedom
    By Kerry Spina

Regular Features

4   Your Letters & Photos

6   Ask Our Expert

30 Your Story

35 Beyond Birth
    By Julia Jones

48 Dad's Corner
    By John Pillinger

59 What's Cooking?
    Spicy Lamb Patties & Sugar Free Banana Cake

65 Mumprenuer Interview
    With Melinda Bito from Eco Toys

69 Activity Time
    By Emily Filmore

70 Organic Gardening: Sowing the
    Seeds of Love
    By Claire Bickle

72 Yoga for Kids: Yoga Sanctuary
    By Kylie DeGiorgio

74 Book Reviews
    by Sharon Dowley

76 Product Reviews

78 What's On
    By Melissa Rogers from A Little Bird

80 Directory

Intellectual Development

32 Unschooling: Inspired Thinking or
    Educational Neglect
    By Chaley Scott

66 A Truely Nurturing Education Part 2
    By Dr Andrew Seaton

Editor's Letter

Nurture
Australia's Natural Parenting Magazine

www.nurtureparentingmagazine.com.au

I recently read an article by Robin Grille called *Parent Guilt: A Silent Epidemic.** It made me realise that I had been carrying around a huge amount of guilt about how I had raised William to date. Essentially my guilt relates to the first three months of William's life (before I allowed myself to trust my instincts). For example, I had guilt that:

- I allowed him to go to sleep by himself (he self-settled from birth believe it or not ~ I actually thought that was a good thing until I read James McKenna's research on co-sleeping!);
- I put him in the co-sleeper next to my bed for three months (rather than in our bed);
- I couldn't let him comfort suck (I had attachment problems and it was too painful). It did not take long for him to find his thumb for comfort ~ which is an everyday reminder for me.

… I think that was it!

I spoke to my husband a few times about how I felt and he would say to me 'You did the best you could with the knowledge you had at the time'. But, as a perfectionist, that just didn't cut it. It didn't alleviate my guilt. Then along came Grille's article – like it was written just for me! He explained that there is a difference between guilt and remorse. He wrote that guilt is *'self-focused – and it is about*

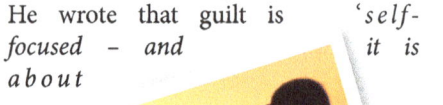

beating ourselves up. By definition, guilt is the fear of retribution. Guilt gnaws at your guts while it tells you 'look what you've done, what kind of a parent are you? You should have known better!' As a pre-emptive measure against judgment of our peers, guilt strikes the first blow against ourselves'. On the other hand, Grille explains that remorse *'builds love; it heals, it is the very thing that allows us to move on and let go'*.

By shifting my perspective I could heal and build a better relationship with my son. So, while breastfeeding one day I spoke to William about my feelings. I know that he did not understand the words I spoke (he was only 9 months old), but I know that he would have felt the feeling I had. I actually cried during this discussion, which felt like a release. Needless to say, I felt much better. Now, whilst I wish I had of read more natural parenting information before I gave birth, I feel that we are now on the right track (for us!) and I don't carry around that guilt that kept me awake some nights.

I know that I'm not the only one that had this guilt. Parental guilt is everywhere. I'm sure while reading this your mind raised a few little guilts too. If so, feel them, acknowledge them and talk to your child about them and, if your child can talk, listen while your child tells you how they feel about it ~ as that is the only way you can heal and move on to a more rewarding relationship with your child.

So, the second reason for starting the magazine was to provide others with the information I wish I had prior to having William to help them with their parental decisions. Knowing what I know now, I would have co-slept from the start, settled him to sleep every time and obtained lactation help much sooner.

Knowledge is power! So I hope that this is more power to you!

Kristy xo

The article is available on our website:
www.nurtureparentingmagazine.com.au

Editor
Kristy Pillinger

Graphic Design
Karah Edwards

Photography
Anne Higgs Photography & Depositphotos

Issue Contributors
Naomi Aldort, Kelly Bartlett, Kristin Beckedahl, Claire Bickle, Prue Blackmore, Sarah Cody, Kylie De Giorgio, Sharon Dowley, Claire Eaton, Emily Filmore, Lisa Guy, Kate Hale, Bonnie Harris, Julia Jones, Petrea King, Dr. Sarah Lantz, Darren Mattock, Tracey Murkett, Melissa Rogers, Rachel Schofield, Chaley Scott, Dr. Andrew Seaton, Arnaum Walkley, Melanie Wright,

Editorial Enquires:
editor@nurtureparentingmagazine.com.au

Advertising Enquires:
advertise@nurtureparentingmagazine.com.au

Feedback:
feedback@nurtureparentingmagazine.com.au

Subscriptions:
subscribe@nurtureparentingmagazine.com.au

Printed by Webstar
Distributed in Australia by IPS

Nurture is published four times a year (March, June, September and December) by Nurture Parenting Magazine Pty Ltd

No part of this publication may be reproduced in any form whatsoever without the written consent of the publisher.
All rights reserved.

Content within this magazine is information only and not necessarily the views of the editor. It is not meant to be a substitute for professional medical advice. Please consult your healthcare provider if you are in any doubt regarding any of this information.

A baby carrier should do more than just look good

Your baby loves being snuggled close to you. In fact, studies show carried babies spend longer in a calm, alert state. But some carriers may compromise spine and hip development. A qualified German babywearing instructor designed the **manduca**® baby carrier to ensure your baby's safety and comfort. Baby is carried in the m-position®, where the knees sit higher than the bottom – optimal for hip health. The integrated newborn insert is made of a cooling organic cotton. A zip extends the carrier back to support your growing baby. And the comfort and ergonomic design extends to the wearer too. **manduca** is Australia's superior carrier.

Experience a new era in babywearing with **manduca**. Available at leading baby stores.
www.manduca.com.au

Rated ★★★★★ at mouthsofmums.com.au
and at productreview.com.au

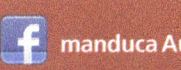 manduca Australia   @ManducaOz   www.fertilemind.com.au

Your Letters

Write to us & WIN!

Email your letters to
editor@nurtureparentingmagazine.com.au

The 'letter of the quarter' will win a selection of 100% certified organic baby products (RRP $49.95)

courtesy of:

I'm not Alone!

I just wanted to say a HUGE thank you for the magazine. It's as if someone has tailor-made a magazine just for me and my parenting style! From the articles about gentle and thoughtful parenting techniques, breastfeeding, chemicals that are in our immediate environment to the product reviews and ads with 'natural' products and cloth nappies. I love it all :) I've read and re-read it all over and over!

It's funny because up until a couple of months ago I felt fairly alone in my parenting style. I just followed my instincts and my heart. I'd never heard of "attachment' or "natural" parenting. I used to get a few strange looks and negative comments from friends, family and "health" professionals for the way I go about raising my son (particularly the co-sleeping). But I've stuck to my guns and I'm so glad I have. Our 10 month son is now such a bright, happy, secure little man!

And now to find a community of like minded people who feel and do things in a similar way to us makes me feel connected and not so alone.

So thank you! I cannot wait to see what the new issue brings! :)

Nakita, mum to Hudson (10mths)

First Issue was a Pleasant Surprise!

I went into my newsagent to buy a greeting card, and decided to look at the parenting magazines. I never end up buying any because I always feel manipulated to buy products, just from reading the covers and having a quick flick through. It just seems like they exist to sell me more stuff; articles included. Then I saw Nurture on the shelf. I'd never heard of it, even through my natural parenting connections, so didn't know what to expect. I was delighted that the articles actually were written to give me information and empower me as a parent, not to make me feel like I'm not good enough because my child doesn't have this thing or that! Congratulations on a fantastic publication! I can't wait for the next issue.

Amy, mum to Grace (6), Naomi (4) and Joshua (3mths)

I'm more Confident now!

Thank you so much for this magazine. It is amazing. I am currently 6 months pregnant with my first child and do not have a lot of friends with children to relate to and to ask questions.

Since I have been pregnant I have had so many people trying to tell me that I 'have to get our baby immunised', 'co sleeping is bad', 'don't pick them up to much', 'you have to smack them or they get out of control' ect. It is such a relief to know that my partner and I are not alone and that there are other parents out there that have/are raising their children naturally and that it has worked. I also have been trying to find the best organic baby products and I was unsure as I don't always trust what the packaging says. You have also helped me out a lot with this.

Thank you so much again I feel a lot more confident in my choice parenting style. I cant wait to read the next issue!
Erin, pregnant

Fabulous Magazine!

I was so excited to receive the first copy of Nurture magazine; it looks fabulous! What an impressive publication. From the technical aspects like layout and paper stock to the artistic presentation and article content, everything about this magazine is so high-quality. And a huge thank you for publishing information about how to help families develop positive relationships. I absolutely cannot wait to read the next issue!
Kelly, (USA) mum to 2 children

Your Photos

Below: Sol (14 months) wearing his amber necklace and loving the great outdoors!

Above: Declan (6 months) having some of mumma's milk

Above right: Archie (18 months) and Willow (20 months) loving their old fashioned play!

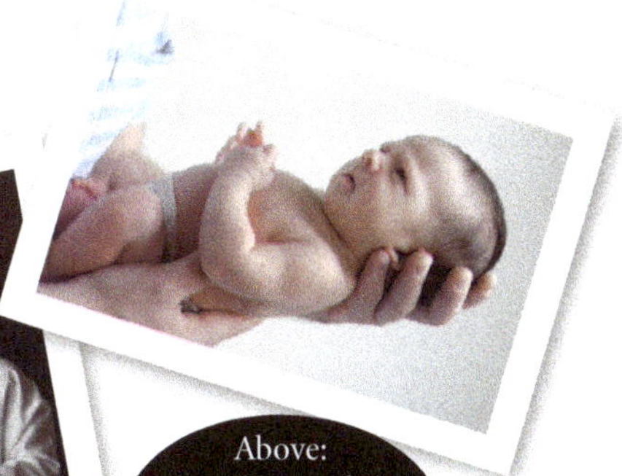

Above: Levi (2 months) getting to know his surroundings

Editor's family photos: Below left: My dad at 18 months; Below right: Me, my dad, brother & sister 30 years ago!

Send us your photos & WIN

E-mail your photos to editor@nurtureparentingmagazine.com.au
The 'photo of the quarter' will win a $60 voucher to spend at

Baby Chilli

www.babychilli.com.au

10% OFF for Nurture readers Code: Nurture1

For the best nature has to offer

Natural. Organic. Safe.

Natural Babycare
Nurture & Nourish with Nature

Natural products for baby, mum & home

www.NaturalBabycare.com.au

www.facebook.com/NaturalBabycare
www.pinterest.com/NaturalBabycare

Ask our Experts

Q I have a daughter who is almost two. I'm all about accentuating the positive and it's worked wonders with our dog. But it's not as easy with a strong willed toddler. How do we get her to not do things like throwing food off the table or climbing on the dining table etc. I really need some practical advice?

A Children respond positively when we communicate at their level, and have expectations that match their abilities. Focusing on your daughter's 'positive' behaviours will help her understand your expectations. A few practical things you can do are discussed below:

Communicate with more than Words

Adults often think that using dialogue is enough to get the message across; tone, pitch and body language. However, whilst they are very important, it may still fall on deaf ears. This is because they want to do things their way, it is fun and they receive lots of attention.

Another form of communication that can also be effective is touch. For example:
- If you are not quick enough to prevent her climbing on the table, step in immediately and take her off.
- Physically remove her from the situation, and change the dynamics.
- Hold her on your lap, look into her eyes and tell her what you expect of her simply and specifically using a deep, firm voice (I refer to this change in tone and pitch as the 'serious voice'. When you change your tone it will help attract her attention).

Life is a Game

Toddlers are very self-absorbed, busy and think the world revolves around them; everything is a game. You can use this to your advantage. For example to help her to discern the difference between play time and meal times:
- Use games and role playing to teach.
- Role play with teddy, showing her how to sit still and enjoy her food.
- Ensure you factor in one on one play time a few times every day, so her 'Love Cup' is full.
- Allow her the opportunity to get messy during the day with play dough, mud and paint instead of food.

Child Friendly Meal Times

To make meal time more child friendly for your daughter, try:
- Using a small table and chairs.
- As her role model, sit down with her at the table and eat at the same time.
- A plastic tablecloth on the floor will help with mess containment.
- Perhaps use this time to read a story or interact with her in another way.
- Toddlers also tend to graze, so offering more nutritious smaller meals may suit.

Age Appropriate Behaviour

Although we all want our child to act reasonably, we must consider whether we are requiring behaviour that is age appropriate. For example:
- A toddler's concentration span is short; expecting a child to sit still for more than 10 minutes is a stretch and can result in undesired behaviour. This is especially the case if a child previously roamed around while eating as it can take a while to learn a new skill
- Toddlers are messy when eating (although at 2, this is not 'throwing food')

The goal is to have your child sitting still and focusing on enjoying her food, without stress or a power struggle.

Being two is still very new; there is so much to learn. With a loving touch, a firm 'serious voice', eye contact and clear specific directions she will learn to focus better when listening to you.

Practise patience, while focusing on what you desire and she will follow your queue.

Arnaum Walkley is a counsellor, parenting coach and accredited NLP Practitioner. Arnaum runs Parenting Solutions which provides practical effective solutions for everyday parenting problems.

If you have a question for our experts, send it to asknurture@nurtureparentingmagazine.com.au. The featured question will receive a gift pack from Wot Not Naturals valued at $35.80

What will you choose?

nature's child

Cloth
$200+

Ingredients:
Organic Cotton

Disposable
$3000+

Ingredients:
Water   Chemical gels
Paper pulp   Hydrogen-peroxide
Plastic

Do you know the real cost of every day products?

Cloth $ in a 3yr period per child

Nappies	$200 - 800	Water, Electricity	
Nappy Wipes	$90	Detergents	$500
Breast Pads	$50		
Face Wipes	$75		
Change mats	$30		
Swimmers	$30		
Bibs	$50		

Totals $1000+

Disposable $ in a 3 year period per child

Nappies	$3000 – 4000 (depending on brand)
Nappy Wipes	$1000
Breast Pads	$250
Face Wipes	$500
Change mats	$500
Swimmers	$300
Bibs	$300

Totals $6000+

NB: note rubbish collection rates are not included and may be extra

Ever noticed how much having a baby costs? We can help you save thousands of dollars by using the very best quality for your baby. Certified Organic Cotton nappies, baby wipes, body creams and swimmers cost you much less than the disposable equivalents. It's good health sense, great environmental sense and amazing value for you!

Shop at our website **www.natureschild.com.au** or phone for your nearest stockist
Mention Nurture Magazine and we will send you a **FREE** Money Saving Info Pack and product sample.
PHONE 1300 555 632 or email orders@natureschild.com.au to collect yours now!

5 Ways to Encourage (Rather than Praise)

'Good boy' or 'good girl' seems to roll off the tongue for many parents. However, what if there was something better you could say? Something more meaningful? **Kelly Bartlett** *explains why praise should be interchanged with encouragement and provides five examples of encouraging phrases*

It's no secret that kids need encouragement to thrive. But what exactly does encouragement sound like? It's different than praise or admiration or guidance. It is common to want to give evaluative feedback to children for their work ("Good coloring!"), or to tell them what we like about their accomplishments ("I like how you set the table."), or what we expect of their behaviour ("You need to try your best at school today.") Though these kinds of responses are well meaning, they teach children to rely on our evaluations rather than to learn to form their own judgments about behaviour.

Alfie Kohn, researcher and author of *Punished by Rewards*, says that children can come to depend on praise and external validation instead of finding satisfaction in doing the right thing simply because it's the right thing to do. "Rather than bolstering a child's self-esteem, praise may increase a child's dependence on us. It leads them to measure their worth in terms of what will lead us to smile and dole out some more approval," says Kohn. He recommends that parents focus on supporting and encouraging their child's efforts, rather than on praising the results.

Encouragement is about teaching children to see the value of their own accomplishments and to be in charge of their own success. It fosters internal strength and motivation by keeping the focus of children's behavior on themselves instead of anyone else. As psychologist Rudolf Dreikurs said, "A child needs encouragement like a plant needs water." Here are five encouraging things to say to your children on a regular basis:

1. "THANK YOU!"

For tasks that a child has completed, let him know his efforts are appreciated. Tell him, "That helped a lot," and, "I appreciate the time you spent on this." It lets him know that his work is meaningful and he is an important contributor to the family. Saying 'thank

> **Five Phrases to Encourage your Child:**
> 1. Thank You!
> 2. You Did It!
> 3. I'm Listening
> 4. It's OK to Cry
> 5. I Trust You

you' is no less celebratory than saying 'good job.' Expressing gratitude for a job well done still communicates excitement and pride. The difference is you don't need to tell your child that what he did was good; he will inherently feel it.

Claire, a stay-at-home mum of 3 boys, said that at dinner one night, she thanked her 3-year-old, Tucker, for giving each family member a napkin to use. When Tucker climbed into his chair and replied, "Mama, I like you thanking me. That feels nice," she was struck by the power of those simple words. Without any praise, Tucker felt significant and appreciated; he felt his "good job," and he was motivated to do it again.

2. "YOU DID IT!"

Use this kind of encouragement for when a child has achieved a goal or milestone. Cheer for her by focusing on the effort it took to get there, rather than on the outcome. Instead of saying, "I like how you built that Lego tower," respond with, "Wow you worked hard on that!", "Look at what you accomplished!", or, "You must feel proud." Responses like these focus the accomplishment on the child's inner work, rather than on a parent's external evaluation. It's much more encouraging to say, "You sure never gave up during your game!" than, "You won your game, good job."

3. "I'M LISTENING."

What could be more encouraging than to know someone is receptive to what you have to say? Active listening validates a child's sense of significance and belonging in the family; they know they're important and they matter. Let your children know you're taking their thoughts seriously by echoing their statements back to them. There should be some back-and-forth with open-ended questions ("What would you do about that?"), empathy ("Wow, you must have felt scared."), and reflections ("Oh, you decided to take a break so you could calm down.") Good listening sounds more like a conversation than a one-sided monologue. When a child is heard, she feels known.

4. "IT'S OK TO CRY."

It's important for children to know that their feelings are always OK. Learning how to manage these feelings takes support, acceptance, and lots of practice. Encourage children by communicating that they are not wrong to experience unpleasant feelings like sadness, anger, or fear. Instead of saying, "You're OK. Don't be upset," let your child know, "You have the right to feel angry. I understand; I would feel mad, too." Or, "I can see you feel very sad right now, and that's OK." Validating your child's feelings leads to his own acceptance of them, and the realisation that he is capable of handling them.

5. "I TRUST YOU."

Instead of providing the answers and directing children toward what to do, encourage them to make decisions and solve problems by letting them know you trust their ability to decide for themselves. Say things like, "I know you can figure this out," "I have faith in you to find a solution," "I know you'll make an appropriate decision," or "You lead the way on this." Entrusting children to make their own decisions is very empowering for young children! It shifts the dynamic from a parent's control over a child to one of shared control. It encourages children to think through problems and come up with their own solutions.

Remember that by opting for encouragement over praise, you're not ignoring your children's accomplishments or successes. Encouragement is simply about keeping your response focused on their efforts and feelings as opposed to only the outcomes. Encouraging words not only reassure children during times of success ("Wow, that took a lot of concentration!"), but also in times of disappointment ("I have faith in you to fix this mistake."). Instead of looking to a parent for affirmation, children are able to decide how they feel about themselves. Their failures and successes, as they should be, are about them, not anyone else.

Kelly Bartlett is a Certified Positive Discipline Educator, Attachment Parenting Leader, and mother of two. You can find more of her work at www.kellybartlett.net

Toxic Toys

Plastic toys seem to be the norm for children these days. From plastic rattles to plastic bikes and doll houses. However, plastic toys may be quite harmful for your child. **Dr Sarah Lantz** *shares the chemicals and toxins that may be found in your child's plastic toys.*

There is something intuitive about children such that they opt to play with wrapping paper and cardboard boxes instead of the plastic toys contained inside the present. Jedda, my two-year old daughter, enjoys shredding wrapping paper and running her little fingers over the silky ribbons. She likes texture. Adiva, now nearly 7, spends hours in cardboard boxes pretending she's a cheetah. We have been known to feed the wild animal inside the box, only for her to growl back.

Play is at the heart of talking about 'toys'. And play is important at all ages. It is literally a biological imperative. Children learn about themselves and their world through play - developing cognitive and problem-solving skills, personal and social skills, physical development. Play stimulates the senses and invigorates the mind. And yet, for the last century we have been endorsing large quantities of mass-produced, low quality, automated, plastic, disposable toys. And what's the problem with this?

Along with the choking and stragulation hazards, massive toy recalls, excessively loud toys, projectile toys, toys that distract and over stimulate, there are a range of toxic chemicals in toys. And as a public health researcher and mama, it is these toxic chemicals that are the focus of my research and heart of this article.

PLASTIC – NOT SO FANTASTIC (POLYVINYL CHLORIDE)

Polyvinyl chloride (also known as PVC or vinyl) is a plastic chemical used in toy production. And its nasty stuff. Every stage in PVC's life cycle involves the production, use, and release of toxic chemicals, with some of the culprits including dioxin, mercury, lead, cadmium, organotins, and phthalates. Because these chemicals are not tightly bound to the plastic, they can enter children's bodies when the children chew or suck on the toys or the PVC packaging that the toys come in. These chemicals are all toxic to children when ingested. And there is no safe way to manufacture, use, or dispose of PVC products.

'Along with the choking and strangulation hazards, massive toy recalls, excessively loud toys, projectile toys, toys that distract and over stimulate, there are a range of toxic chemicals in toys'

In 2008, one of the largest toy manufactures in the world, Toys R Us, made a promise to reduce the use of PVC plastic in the toys they sell and offer more safer PVC-free products. But Toys R Us have not kept their promise. A report released two years later, entitled Toxic Toys 'R' Us, by the Centre for Health, Environment and Justice (CHEJ), found that Toys R Us continue to sell toys made with PVC – and lots of it. Almost 70 different toys, including well-known brands were tested. According to the report:

- 72.5 percent of all toys/children's products tested contained high levels of chlorine, indicating they were likely made of PVC.
- 20.3 percent of all toys/children's products tested contained tin, indicating the likely presence of organotins in these toys.
- 52.9 percent of all toy packaging tested contained high levels of chlorine, indicating they were likely made of PVC.
- 52.9 percent of all toy packaging tested contained tin, indicating the likely presence of organotins.
- Only one of the 70 products that we tested was labeled as containing PVC.
- 81 percent toys ofmarketed to infants and toddlers 18-36 months and up in age contained chlorine, indicating they were likely made of PVC.
- 19 percent of these toddler-targeted toys contained tin, indicating the likely presence of organotins in these toys.

Toys that tested positive for PVC included well known toys such as Barbie, 'Toys Story 3' Woody and Buzz Lightyear figures, Disney Princess dolls, Zhu Zhu Pets, Nickelodeon's Dora the Explorer and Diego figures, Club Penguin figurines, Imaginext toddler action figures and many others, from dolls and balls, to baby bath time toys and products, and even some children's Sippy Cups.

Another report released in 2011 by the International Persistent Organic

Pollutants (POPs) Elimination Network (IPEN) and based in the Philippines found many children's toys have dangerously high levels of heavy metals. The international study measured toxic metals in 200 children's products with a focus on antimony, arsenic, cadmium, chromium, lead, and mercury. Approximately 30% of the products contained at least one toxic metal above acceptable levels. 37 products (19%) contained lead at or above the Australian regulatory limit, and children's toy cosmetics contained mercury levels 4 – 5 times higher than the regulatory limit. Given that the toy market is global, children all across the world, including Australian children, can be directly affected by these toys.

But isn't there a regulatory agency for toys made, or imported, into Australia?

The regulation of toxic chemicals in toys in Australia is still sketchy at best. The Australian Toy Standard have been established, but these standards are voluntary, so there are no requirements for toy manufacturers and distributors to abide by them. Compliance essentially relies on voluntary testing. This is also the case for toys imported into Australia. Hazardous toys can only be detected by testing and analysing toy components, and given the large volume and range of toys imported into Australia, this prohibits Customs routinely testing all imported toys. In light of this, parents need to be diligent. And these are the reasons why…

There are no safe levels of lead and mercury for children. Lead directly attacks the nervous system and destroys brain cells. Mercury causes both chronic and acute poisoning, damages the brain and significantly disrupts hormones. Dioxin, a byproduct of PVC manufacturing (usually produced when burning chlorine), and is a group of persistent toxic chemicals. While children are not exposed to dioxin when they handle toys or toy packaging, dioxin is released into the environment

dragonflytoys.com.au
keeping the magic of childhood alive...

natural + ethically made toys, clothing, arts + crafts for babies + children
store: dragonfly toys at organic feast 10 william street east maitland nsw

during both the manufacturing and disposal of PVC materials. Dioxin then gets into our water ways and food production systems. Children consume dioxin from meat, fish, diary products and eggs. Dioxin is a potent cancer causing agent, and has reproductive (decreased fertility, endometriosis, decreased sperm counts, birth defects etc.), developmental, immunological, and endocrine health impacts.

PHTHALATES

Phthalates (Pronounced THA-lates) are chemicals added to plastic toys to soften them, fix scent in fragrances, and colour personal care and cosmetics, including children's face paints. While Phthalates are no longer manufactured in Australia, around two million tons of phthalates are produced across the world each year, with more than 20 types of phthalates imported and commonly used in Australian toys. The total amount of phthalate contained in a toy product varies from about 10 to 50%, depending on the degree of softness required.

A growing body of research reveals that exposure to phthalates and their metabolites can cause a range of health impacts. Phthalates exposure has been linked to:
- Interference with the natural functioning of the hormone system
- Asthma and other respiratory problems, rhinitis and eczema in children
- Reproductive and genital defects
- Premature birth and early onset of puberty
- Risk factors for testicular cancer
- Increased incidence of congenital genital malformations and spermatogenic dysfunction.

A 2012 study also suggested that high levels of phthalates may be connected to the current obesity epidemic in children.

Infants are exposed to phthalates from multiple sources including through the umbilical cord, breast milk, dust in the air and also from sucking or mouthing PVC plastic toys. And the cumulative impact of different phthalates leads to an exponential increase in associated harm.

The European Union (EU) introduced temporary bans on phthalates in children's toys as far back as 1999. The EU has phased out the use of three phthalate plasticisers in toys and child-care items, and they will be permanently phased out by the EU by February 2015:
- Di(2-ethylhexyl)phthalate (DEHP)
- Di-n-butyl phthalate (DBP)
- Benzyl butyl phthalate (BBP)
- The EU further restricts three plasticisers from toys and childcare items that children can put in their mouths:
- Diisononyl phthalate (DINP)
- Diisodecyl phthalate (DIDP)
- Di-n-octyl phthalate (DNOP)

In 2010 Australia banned Diethylhexyl Phthalate (DEHP) in products used by children up to and including 36 months of age. While the Australian Competition and Consumer Commission (ACCC) continues to collaborate with our chemical regulatory boards to monitor international research into phthalates, and may take specific regulatory action to address risks to people associated with the use of phthalates in consumer products, Australian standards significantly lags behind international standards. Therefore, while phthalates all have complex chemical names, it's important to be able to identify some of the key ones to avoid exposing your children to.

ARSENIC

Many kids climbing structures – with their wooden gangways, turrets, and tunnels – are still made out of pressure-treated lumber (copper chrome arsenate - CCA) which contain arsenic – a notoriously deadly poison and established human carcinogen. While in 2006 the Australian Pesticides and Veterinary Medicines Authority (APVMA) restricted the use of treated timber used in 'intimate human contact' applications such as children's play equipment, furniture, residential decking and hand-railing, it did not recommend dismantling or removing of existing treated wood structures, so many still exist. Authorities have been remiss in not carrying out soil or wipe test in children's playgrounds.

There is a list of matters to consider when buying your children toys. However, there is no better toy than nature. As a mumma I watch how my children, and other children, connect with nature with such ease and grace if we give them the space to do so. It's like breathing to them. John Muir's quote is apt here:

'When one tugs at a single thing in nature, (s)he finds it attached to the rest of the world'

Dr Sarah Lantz is a mama, writer, and researcher from Queensland University of Technology with a background in public and population health and author of the bestselling book Chemical Free Kids; Raising healthy Children in a Toxic World. www.chemicalfreeparenting.com.au or www.nontoxsoapbox.com

TOXIC FREE TOY SELECTION

It is of no surprise that an increasing number of parents are seeking more natural toys for their children. Consider what it is that makes a good toy, a toy that is suited to the age of the child, and also your own families' philosophies and health priorities. Here are a few suggestions:

- Choose age-specific toys. Remember that babies and toddlers can be oral with their play and will suck and chew on just about anything to learn about their environment.

- Avoid vinyl and PVC toys such as bath toys, squeeze toys, dolls, lunch boxes and drink bottles. Instead, choose plastic-free toys such as certified organic fabric teethers and wooden toys (unpainted preferably unless you know about the paint source).

- Beware of 'cheap' children's jewellery and check whether parts are PVC, pewter alloys, or lower-grade tins. Painted beads may also contain lead. Consider making your own creations with natural materials such as wood, hemp, seeds, crystals and shells.

- Try plant-based natural make-up for children's face painting and dress-ups. These are made of vegetable oils, beeswax, carnauba, and mineral pigments.

- Read labels of children's cosmetics carefully and avoid nail polish and other products such as perfumes, hair products and fake tattoos.

- Seek assurances and testing from the manufacturers, importers or retailers of painted or metal toys to avoid lead and other heavy metal contaminants.

- Toys made from natural materials are everywhere and sometimes do not have to be bought at all - blank paper and natural paints; wooden blocks; sand; pots and pans; boxes of clothes for dress-up; clay; material and fabric; gardening tools; outdoor riding and climbing toys such as a wagon, a ladder, or hanging bars; and common household items that children may have access to when they want to imitate household activity, such as cooking, cleaning, nurturing, fixing, and building tools.

Consider also that nature is the best toy of all. Children, more than ever before, are disconnected from nature – have reduced amounts of leisure time; spend more time in front of the TV and computerized toys; are over stimulated yet live more sedentary lifestyles than ever before. Richard Louv calls this phenomenon 'nature deficit disorder'. Consider that it is in our best interest to reconnect to nature, not only because aesthetics or justice demands it, but because our mental, physical, and spiritual health depends upon it. Exposure to nature reduces diseases, improves cognitive abilities, and resistance to stresses. The health of the earth also depends upon it as well. How children connect with nature, and how we, as parents raise our children, will shape the conditions of future cities, homes, parks and the conditions of our animals, plants and ecosystems.

Conscious Parenting: What's & Why's

*New styles of parenting seem to pop up every few minutes. However, one important new style is called 'conscious parenting'. **Prue Blackmore** explains what conscious parenting is and why many parents have implemented this style of parenting*

A lot of work has been done over time on what it is to be a child and what it is to be a parent however what makes a conscious parent is the nature of the relationship that exists between the two.

Conscious parenting is a healing activity in which everyday tasks and interactions become the very medium for emotional and spiritual growth. Most of us grew up in a world where well meaning and well intentioned people gave us a story about who we are and what kind of life we will live, for no other reason but because that was what was done to them. The way we parent is powerfully influenced by the way we were parented.

Every human is unique and every relationship is filled with more possibilities for growth than we may ever realize. We live in an imperfect world and were parented imperfectly and will repeat this with our children, until we stop and consciously decide we want more for our children, than what we grew with.

This is not to criticize our care givers, for in the vast majority of cases they did the best that they could with what they had - but that does not necessarily mean it was good for us. Often they handed on the unresolved conflicts and wounds from their own childhood and people then spend the rest of their lives struggling with these issues and trying to recover from them.

People come together as adults for survival, hoping their partners will meet the unmet needs of childhood. This is appropriate. Children are often produced unconsciously to meet these needs as well and this places an impossible and intolerable burden upon the child, one that they will spend their lives trying to resolve, for they are not equipped to meet our needs in this way.

It can set up a life time pattern of fear of failure, guilt and anxiety, feelings of inadequacy, simply because they could not do, what they were not equipped to do. This is normal. The World Health Organisation estimates that over 90% of the human population exists this way – but normal does not mean healthy.

With the birth of a child, parents experience what it is like to love completely and unconditionally and this

> *'When we become conscious we understand that our child is born whole, and that it is possible to preserve this wholeness while they are under our care.'*

is usually for the first time and ensures the survival of the young and the species. In the presence of an infant we are open to the philosopher Martin Buber's thoughts on the sacredness of everyday life. We feel the connection between ourselves and the rest of creation.

Our job is to experience oneness with the child while helping them to grow into an independent functioning adult, while honouring and appreciating the differences between us. Each child is born with a combination of potential and limitation that forms their temperament. The interactions they have, first with us and then with society, will influence how the personality develops from this. The role of the parent is to maximize the positive environmental factors and to help recover from the negative ones.

When we become conscious we understand that our child is born whole, and that it is possible to preserve this wholeness while they are under our care. We can become self reflective and initiate the changes we need to make in our lives, to heal ourselves and in doing this we ensure our children have the best chance in the world to become themselves and fulfill the promise of their birth.

If we want to take better care of our children we need to take better care of ourselves. Our maturity and intelligence - emotional, psychological and spiritual - will be reflected in the children we raise. Having a child is a once in a lifetime opportunity to heal childhood wounds and become whole ourselves – through the self revelation that occurs during parenting. The problems you may be having with your child offers invaluable information about what parts of you are unfinished or incomplete as a result of your own childhood. Your efforts to become a conscious parent will have a profound effect on your child and this will be handed onto their children and down on the line.

A child is born into wholeness until it is taken away. It is important to stop and see the child as it is, someone who is living authentically, in the moment,

unfiltered - in ways that we have long forgotten.

Our emotional reactions to a child are feedback from ourselves to ourselves. If it is a negative emotional reaction, it is telling us that the way we are approaching the issue is not working, and is in fact coming from a wounded part of ourselves - thus not being about the child.

When the child is resisting the way we parent, that is feedback from them to us – as is positive compliance to a request – and they show us what works. A child's only desire is to please you, it is all they want. So when there is conflict it is usually about the way we are going about it.

When you step back and give yourself permission to see the child as a teacher – you have taken the first step to release yourself from old patterns. Learn to see the child as they are, rather than as you think they should be and see the child that you have, rather than the one that you think you should have.

Pain is self-centered. It will do anything to protect itself, including sacrificing the needs of its own child. It closes in on itself and blocks reception to outside information. A false self is created in a false world – masks are created and lens of perception are made up to hide the pain and life is lived through this instead of as it is.

This pain becomes so intolerable to a child, that by the age of 7 most children have left their bodies and this everyday precious moment in which we exist and have entered their minds. Here they tend to dwell in the past, worrying about what they did wrong and feeling bad for doing it, or in the future, worrying about how to avoid further pain, guilt, blame and shame.

It stunts a child's impulse to wholeness in order to make them more acceptable to a stunted [and normal] parent. If you are reading this article it is because you want to do it differently than to the way it was done with you and that is a powerful first step - to be congratulated.

Over the ensuing editions we will talk very specifically about what this looks like and offer practical and useful ways of understanding the conflict or behaviour problems you may be wrestling with and how to resolve them but here are some basic first steps.

Prue Blackmore has over 30 years experience as a RN in psychiatry and mental health, and has specialised in developmental psychiatry, child and adolescent psychiatry, cognitive behavioural therapy, transpersonal counselling and trauma resolution

Activities to help you become a more conscious parent

1. **Discover your child** – educate yourself about the basic developmental stages of what your child is doing at different ages and stages. Know what they go through – this is all well documented now and will prevent you expecting things of them that they are not neurologically wired for yet.

2. **Identify your parenting style** – there are only two in this model – are you an 'imploder' or an 'exploder' and what is your partner? Parents tend to have the same wounds but a lock and key approach. In other words you will work opposite to each other often and this polarises you both causing conflict and puts the child in the middle.

3. **You are not your child** – imperative – let go of symbiosis or enmeshment with your child. You need to feel this one in your bones. Without this, your unmet needs from your own childhood will intrude into the relationship with your child and recreate the wound.

4. **Understand yourself** – get feedback; this can be difficult as we defend ourselves, but is very useful, we all have blind spots. What are the patterns, the conflicts, the discomforts? Where you are stuck, will cause you difficulty in helping your child navigate the same areas.

5. **Identify your core beliefs** – your script messages. What is it to be a good parent, what are your 'shoulds'? Without awareness you will act them out no matter what it may cost your child.

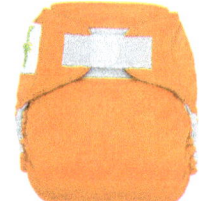

HEALTH UPDATE: Springtime Allergies

Nareen Bizzell, a naturopath from Yin Health on the Sunshine Coast, discusses how best to deal with springtime allergies

As the weather warms up again and we pack our winter woollies away for another year, many of us look forward to the enjoying the spring sunshine and heading back outdoors for fun activities with our family and friends. And while most of us enjoy this time of year, it is certainly not the case for the huge number of seasonal allergy sufferers out there.

Seasonal allergies, also known as "hay fever" or seasonal allergic rhinitis, are a collection of symptoms that occur during certain times of the year which are caused by tree, grass and weed pollens being released into the air. The immune systems of people who are allergic to these particles in the air treat them as invaders and release chemicals, including histamine, into the bloodstream to defend against them. It's the release of these chemicals that causes allergy symptoms.

If you have noticed your child having sneezing fits, rubbing their itchy red eyes and giving you the "allergic salute" (constant nose wiping), it may be that they are suffering from seasonal allergies. So how can you tell the difference between allergies and a cold that's come on late in the season?

Although some of the symptoms such as a blocked nose are the same, seasonal allergies usually last longer than the typical 1-2 weeks of a cold, they tend to reoccur yearly and throughout the season, there is no fever, and sneezing fits and itchy/watery eyes are common.

So what can you as a parent do to help and support your child who may be suffering with allergies? Well there are a lot of lifestyle tips and natural remedies that may provide some relief.

1. Reduce exposure to the allergens. This can be easier said then done, but keeping your child indoors on windy spring days can reduce the amount of pollen etc that they come into contact with. Mid morning is generally the peak time that is best to avoid. Also, not drying your allergy-prone child's clothes on the clothesline can help to, as clothes tend to collect the pollens whilst hanging outdoors.
2. Try irrigating the nasal passages with a saline solution to help with the congestion. There are saline sprays in pharmacies that contain no preservatives and are suitable for both babies and children.
3. Look at your child's diet. Some children that have seasonal allergies also have food intolerances and sensitivities which can increase inflammation and mucous production. The main foods that it can be worth decreasing temporarily to see if it helps are wheat and dairy. Your naturopath can also help you with identifying any potential problem foods.
4. Try natural foods and supplements that have been shown to help. Bioflavonoids can help decrease histamine release and therefore help with the symptoms. Bioflavonoids are found in the pith of citrus fruits, and in most good quality vitamin C powders. Children's strength Fish Oil can also help provide an anti-inflammatory effect, as well as supporting mood and brain function. Homoeopathic formulas can be found at most health food stores, which some parents find to be helpful.
5. See your healthcare practitioner. Your naturopath can assist you by recommending specific practitioner-strength herbs or supplements that will be specific for your child. Your G.P. can also be helpful in identifying allergies by doing skin prick tests.

 For more information, go to www.yinhealth.com

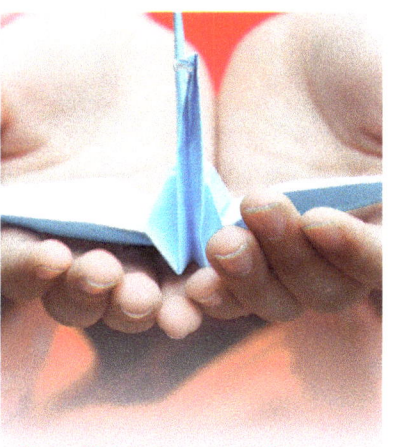

Beautiful baby and children's products all made in Japan

- Baby leg warmers
- Towels
- Cards
- Shinzi Katoh Design
- Zoologique by Tomonori Taniguchi

www.babyconnect.com.au

Can You Hear Me Now?

What parents need to know about their mobile phones

Riley Rose's Story, Age 6

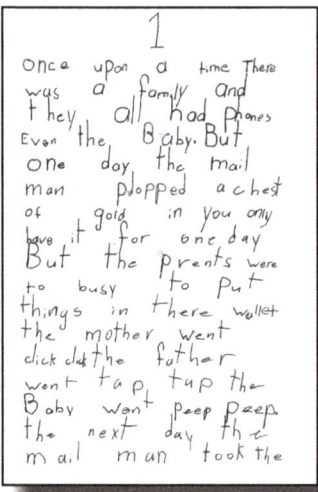

Much has been written about restricting children's screen time, internet access, and video gaming in hope's of insuring their safety and well-being. It's a tough job monitoring our children's activities on screen devices, hoping to protect them from cyberspace predators and bullies. Many parents frantically try to control screen time use fearing video game addictions, no outdoor playtime, and disconnection with the family. Little, however, has been written about the perspective of the child when it is the parents who are unavailable and distant—victims of their own screen dependencies.

THE BRAVE NEW WORLD

Most twenty and thirty-something parents are blithely unaware of how their screen time, especially mobile phone use, affects their children. The use of technological devices is second nature to them and, since they did not experience their own parents' use when they were young, they have no shared experience with their children.

The child's perception of most experiences is often disregarded by parents uneducated in the inner workings of the child's brain and the input of external data on that brain. The developmental stage of egocentrism in the first six years of a child's life, together with an immature prefrontal cortex not yet ready to analyze incoming data, means that the young child takes it like it is.

If dad is on his mobile phone, his preschooler is unable to understand what dad is doing, that it has nothing to do with her, and that he will be with her in a minute or ten. Egocentrism means everything is about me, I am the focus and the cause of everything in my life, hence the message to her is more likely to be, I'm unimportant.

In her story, Riley, who is developmentally on the outside edge of the egocentric stage of her development, is able to see precious opportunities that her parents are missing out on (the pot of gold) by spending time on their mobile phones. Precious time with her. Thus she is missing out on precious time with her parents.

We have a new culture of parents who are accustomed to having the world accessible to them in their pockets. Parents talk or text when they are pushing a stroller, driving a car, supervising playtime, etc., instead of attending to or interacting with their children. Unintentionally the message sent to the child is I'm unavailable. You're on your own. Certainly hovering and over-involvement is not recommended and interferes with growing independence. But when a parent's attention is often taken up with a hand-held screen, and the child more often than not gets a frustrated just a minute response, the child perceives that she is less important than the screen. Is it any wonder children demand attention with louder and more dramatic behaviors meant to draw the parent back in their direction?

Riley's holiday time with her family, as she describes in her story, was blissful with shakes and chocolate and undistracted time with her parents off their devices. Certainly life offers up enough distractions to teach children that their parents have many other jobs in life besides parenting. Do we really want to add our addiction for constant connection to the outside world to their already frustrated attempts to gain our undivided attention?

Hope springs eternal for Riley that upon arrival home to the forgotten phones, her parents will get burned, learn their lesson, and never use them again. What children want more than anything from their parents is time—time that is growing shorter and shorter.

MODELING

No teaching tool is more powerful than modeling. It has been wisely said that we need to be the people we want our children to become. When we are, they will be that and more. Children learn from what we do far more than from what we say.

Being on the phone and unavailable to a child is nothing new. The telephone has brought with it enormous challenges for generations of parents and frustrations for their children who demand attention when their parents are unavailable. What is new is that our phones now go with us everywhere we go. And it's my phone as opposed to the phone. It has become our favorite toy, our most important possession, and a new body part. No wonder even tiny children want to play with them.

It is the job of parents to own and take responsibility for their actions, emotions, and desires and never blame them on their children. "You make me so mad" sends the unintended message that you are responsible for my feelings. "Why do I always have to yell ten times to get you to do what I say?" tells the child that you are responsible for my yelling.

We must also take responsibility for the messages we send our children with our use of tech devices. If our devices are apparently so valuable to us, where can we expect our child's focus to land? What are we modeling for our innocent, egocentric children? Earlier and earlier children are demanding their own mobile phones, iPads, and iPods. 31% of 8 to 10-year-olds have mobile phones. Earlier and earlier children are getting hooked into the unemotional, non-interactive world of cyberspace where anything goes.

TIPS FOR PARENTS' USE

To take control of your modeling, a few simple tips can be the answer:
- Put devices away when you are in the presence of your child.
- If you must have your mobile phone available, keep it on vibrate and check messages later.
- A stay-at-home parent can choose times of the day for use when the child is napping, in school, playing alone or with friends.
- When you go out with your child, leave your mobile phone at home as often as possible.
- If you are on a mobile phone around your child, make sure to use a headset.
- Play video games when your children are sleeping unless you are playing age-appropriate games with them.
- When you must be on your phone or computer, respond with understanding to your child's anger and frustration.

It's simple to take responsibility for damaging modeling that can initiate children to the temptations of the technological world. All it takes is awareness of what you look like to your child on a mobile phone or iPad and setting standards for yourself that will serve as your child's most important teaching.

TAKE RESPONSIBILITY

Pay attention to your mobile phone behavior, take responsibility for how it has affected your child, and change whatever behavior you do not want to see in your child.

It takes empathic observance to see the world from the child's point of view. Most children are not able to directly say, "Mum, I don't like it when you are on your phone and not paying attention to me." But their behavior will tell you if you know how to interpret it. Mostly we just blame our children for bad behavior and pay no attention to what provoked it. Then we get enraged with them, especially teens, when they behave irresponsibly.

If you must use your phone and your child acts out, validate her cues with, "I bet you don't like it when I am on my phone. It must seem like I'm not even here. I promise that if I need to make a call, I will keep it as short as possible. You can come and sit on my lap while I make it." Validation will help your child know that her feelings are appropriate even when she can't get what she wants. We must set the stage now for our child's behavior later.

Riley's parents are lucky to have Riley's perceptive story to clue them in to what her world looks and feels like. Most remain in the dark when attention is on the next text rather than the child's view of Mum texting.

Many parents have addictions or at least dependencies on their mobile phones and other screen devices that create chasms between themselves and their children causing communication breakdown later in the parent/teen relationship when communication is so necessary. Let's make sure we are not sending messages and modeling irresponsible behavior we least intend.

Bonnie Harris director of Connective Parenting and has been a parenting specialist for twenty-five years. She is the author of 'When Your Kids Push Your Buttons' and 'Confident Parents, Remarkable Kids: 8 Principles for Raising Kids You'll Love to Live With'

CHILDREN & MOBILE PHONES

Mobile phones are a way of life and a tremendous convenience and aid. Naturally children want them as soon as possible, and parents rest easier when their children are reachable. Tips on the when and how of getting your child a mobile phone are abundant on the internet. In addition it is imperative to ask yourself some important questions about your role in your child's mobile phone use:

- Are you asking your child to comply with a double standard of do as I say, not as I do?
- Is it okay with you if your child models your mobile phone use?
- Does your child need a mobile phone or want one because everyone else has one?
- Are you able to withstand your child's disappointment if you say no?
- Will your child be self-disciplined enough to follow rules you both agree on or does impulse and temptation still drive his behavior?
- Will your child use the mobile phone to check in with you, ask your advice about something, or let you know her whereabouts or simply text her friends? Does she often borrow someone else's phone to reach you?
- Are you able to educate your child on proper mobile phone etiquette that you back up with your own?
- Will your child use a headset as you do?
- Consider the research from other countries on potential brain damage and make an educated decision

Gender: Do Differences Really Exist?

Do you know if you're having a boy or a girl? The question asked by friends and family when excited couples share their pregnancy news. **Claire Eaton** *shares some of the subtle, yet profound characteristics of boys and girls and how we can embrace them from the moment our little one is born.*

Your baby, do you remember that first precious moment when you saw your baby, you held him against your skin and you made an unconditional and perhaps silent promise to nurture and love him in every way possible? It's in those moments that we are so focused on the health and pure wonder of our baby, that gender seems somewhat irrelevant?

We often find that it isn't until the following months and early years that the gender of our baby seems to have more significance and we want to learn more about the characteristics of our son or daughter throughout their development.

Children who are raised by families who do understand these subtle differences can have an enormous and positive impact on the way their little ones can learn to think, feel, hear, explore and interact with their environment. By sharing some of these unique characteristics, we can better understand our girls and boys. We also bring awareness to any unconscious beliefs about boys and girls that we may have as parents, whilst appreciating our children for their uniqueness rather than creating gender assumptions, competition or comparisons. As we gather more knowledge about our children, we are less likely to incorrectly label our children, see their behaviour as misbehaviour or unfairly compare ourselves to other parents.

"Parents are the active and loving sculptures of their children's growing brains, family experiences that create and shape the biological structures of their child's brain" D. Siegel, MD

YOUR BABY BOY

Research shows that from the moment our boys are born, their right brain (movement, balance and coordination) is more developed than their left (due to the presence of different hormones in the womb). During the first stage of boyhood development 0-6 years, the right brain is specifically responsible for emotions, physical movement and gross motor control; therefore our little boys tend to explore their world in more kinesthetic ways, via physical touch, activity, play and moving things. Their gross muscle skills develop quickly; therefore boys are often inclined to want to express themselves in physical and whole body ways. In addition, boys generally develop their spatial awareness rapidly, which enables them to remember their surroundings, the position of objects, furniture and toys.

Helping our boys be boys

For parents, gender differences are important to know because generally speaking, these signs are the beginning of boys' 'boyishness' and their innate desire to play, rough & tumble, to climb and to test their strength, balance, speed and coordination. Parents who are aware of this and embrace it as a positive aspect of male development, are more able to view these wonderful signs as boys learning about themselves and their world through their body. They are making left and right brain neural connections as they label, describe and interpret their own actions and ability. Unfortunately, boys can be negatively labeled because of their physicalilty and interpreted as 'typical boys' or 'that's boys for you', or 'boys just don't stop'.

Understanding the subtle gender differences better equips us to embrace their boyishness and give them wings to grow into well balanced kids and teens. Sometimes mums find it more challenging to accommodate boys and their traits, whereas dads are sometimes oblivious to it all. Perhaps on a deeper level, males understand what it is that boys are doing and how they are communicating with their body, taking up space, moving in large ways and always 'on the go'.

Keeping right brain dominance in mind, it's absolutely essential that we intentionally help our boys to step out of their physical comfort zone and help them to engage in 'play and chat' times, which are repetitious, where we can gently teach our boys through play, how to connect their left and right brain, enabling their conversation, reasoning and logic skills to develop proportionately.

> *'Both boys and girls need our help from the onset to see their boyishness and girlishness as wonderfully healthy and something to be admired and adored'*

YOUR BABY GIRL

Research shows that from the moment our girls are born, the left side brain is more developed (logic, reasoning, speech). Girl's language and verbal skills can be quicker to develop because the right brain is concerned with logic, reasoning and rational thinking and girls can even gain and maintain eye contact earlier in their infancy. Understanding girls enables us to appreciate their natural desire to chit chat as they grow in to toddlers and preschoolers, wanting to express and interact with the world through conversation, stories and long excited tales.

Helping our girls be girls

Girls become confident in conversation from a very young age, especially as their left brain makes more connections and vocabulary and verbal articulation expands. Bearing this in mind, our girls need our help for them to build their left and right brain and the connection between the two, so with this knowledge, we can provide our daughters with opportunities to use their large muscles groups, communicate through movement and develop their spatial awareness. Through play, fun and safe opportunities, girls can learn and explore whilst developing their right brain skills.

Inherently, mothers often seem to understand girls and their traits who show this left brain dominance and rarely view it as a problem or something that needs to be suppressed or changed, however males can be challenged by this. Cast back to the subtle boy traits; boys and men tend to connect more physically, girls and women more naturally communicate with words and emotions. Encouraging our little girls to continue to explore and have fun with language is great; however, we can also encourage our girls to exercise their right brain in gentle ways, especially through play and games.

Both boys and girls need our help from the onset to see their boyishness and girlishness as wonderfully healthy and something to be admired and adored. Boys and girls who are totally accepted and encouraged to be their gender without competition or comparison are given the gift of opportunity to spread their wings and follow their dreams from toddlers to teens and beyond.

Gender traits and generalisations are merely guides which help us to better connect, understand and tune in to our children; however no girl or boy is quite like your child. He is unique and wonderful, she is amazing and magnificent.

Claire Eaton is a parenting specialist, key note speaker, eBook author of Harmonious Homes & ROC Kids and you can find more of her work at www.creativeparenting.co

Photos: Anne Higgs Photography

Boy Stuff & Girl Stuff CD
gently exploring subtle differences in the world of boys and girls.

All Nurture readers can enjoy a **15% discount**
Just quote promo code "CREATIVE"
Free postage Australia wide.

Visit us at **www.creativeparenting.co**

Creative Parenting
Happy parents. Strong relationships. Thriving children.

15% OFF!

Fatherhood:
Joys & Challenges in the Early Days

New dads can find it hard to know what to do and how to help when bringing home their new bundle of joy. Some tend to stand aside while the women huddle around. **Darren Mattock** *provides some wonderful information on how you can be a more confident 'hands on' dad and partner in the early days.*

Dads have the capacity to do much better than merely "survive" the early days. Every man, with the support and encouragement of the mother of his newborn child, can thrive as a dad.

From my own experience as a father and in my work with expectant and new dads, what I have identified as the key to thriving is a sense of empowerment. This is the gateway to a father stepping in to his new role with a clear sense of purpose, developing a deep bond with his child, and being a supportive partner, as well as a responsible team parent.

I'm a wild idealist by nature, but not wild enough to believe that the early days of fatherhood are simply joyous. They're not! There are brand new life and relationship challenges to manage, and it's a time of radical change and adjustment. However, a sense of empowerment in your role as dad, and a deep connection to your partner and your child that comes from being an involved father, will be solid foundations that you can safely lean upon when faced with the most challenging moments.

There are countless simple, precious, and pure moments of joy to be experienced in the early days. Nothing can change a man more profoundly and spontaneously than his own newborn child; a new love has been born inside of his chest, and a new light shines in his Universe. Be there, in body, mind and spirit, as much as possible, to share in these moments, as they are Fatherhood gold.

Now it's my joy and challenge to share a glimpse of what the early days look and feel like from a father's perspective. Before I do, I wish to acknowledge the fact that every dad will develop his own father role, and in that sense, every dad is unique. This diversity of dad styles is to be celebrated. Every dad wants to be the best father he can so that his child can also thrive – the best way he can achieve that is to authentically be himself.

So, what I humbly aspire to do is plant a few seeds of inspiration of what empowered and involved fatherhood means to you so that you can prepare to create your own father role consciously, with purpose, and develop your own dad style with confidence.

'Every man, with the support and encouragement of the mother of his newborn child, can thrive as a dad.'

THE FIRST WEEK

The first week is one time as a man that you are called upon to seriously multi-task. It commands your full presence and will challenge you in ways you've never experienced. So be prepared!

This is the time when your instinctive protector is called upon for duty. Naturally, your family and friends will want to swoop in on your new arrival and bask in the glow of the miracle of new life with you. This can be incredibly overwhelming! Mum will be feeling exhausted after giving birth and like you, coming to grips with her new role and challenges. The first days at home in your natural environment are foundational for bonding with baby; mum and baby need plenty of quiet and privacy to just be. Therefore, your role is to be the gatekeeper to your mum and bub. Essentially, that means you need to manage the flow of family and friends into your sacred space and what happens in the space.

I encourage you and your partner to have a conversation that is focused on sharing your hopes, needs and expectations of this first week, and agreeing on a plan that is best for your family. Ask your partner all the questions you need to ask so that you have a clear understanding of what her hopes, needs and expectations are. This will ensure that you play your role successfully.

New dads are proud! Father pride rooted in love is a wonderful energy to be in the presence of. You'll want to talk about and share this momentous occasion in your life. Something I encourage you as a new dad to do is share the birth story from your perspective, in your words. Often, new dads will learn the narrative of their partner's version birth story from listening to her share it, and unconsciously share it as their birth story. It's amazing what becomes conscious and is shared during this process; it's a rare emotion-charged moment that is often illuminated with joy. Fatherhood is a rite of passage that is to be honoured and celebrated. The creation of a narrative that is your own is a pivotal moment of embracing your role as a dad and paradigm shift in you being a dad; you step beyond simply being an observer of the birth of your child and empower yourself to be the father who was present at the birth of your child.

The truly joyous moments of the first week are the quiet, private spaces when it is just mum, dad and baby; savour every moment! It's a time when you and your partner, as new parents, are discovering who has been gifted to you. The more time that you have just to be together, the more you will learn and discover about who your baby is. Likewise, the more your baby will get to learn and discover who you are, too.

Now is the best time to initiate your self into the role of a hands-on dad. Dads are equally capable at being hands-on parents in the early days as mums are – the roles and responsibilities are just different. Start changing nappies now. Start bathing your baby now. Start changing your baby's clothes now. Learn what and where everything "baby" is now. Empower yourself as a dad. See your hands-on role as an opportunity to build a relationship with your child. Be lovingly courageous in chartering this unknown territory and as you discover how to tune into and trust your instincts.

It's not all about baby; while being a hands-on dad will provide some much appreciated support to your partner, she also needs to be nurtured and cared for. Your partner will be depending on you for emotional support and practical support, so I encourage you to be fully present with her so that you can best respond to her calling. This may be challenging while you're juggling other roles and callings, but stay connected, keep talking, keep sharing, and keep listening.

One such calling you should be prepared for is supporting your partner as she experiences the 'baby blues'. In the wake of the exhilaration and exhaustion of birth, your partner will be in a vulnerable and raw physical, emotional and psychological state. She may become easily teary, seem flat or even appear to be depressed. The last thing you should do is panic, get scared and back off. What she really needs you to do is step in. Don't take it personally. Be gentle with your words and in your actions. Be affectionate. Hold her. Reassure her. Let her know that you are right there with her, in every way, on every level, so that she feels safe and accepted as she rebalances within her self and begins to come to terms with her new role.

WEEKS TWO - SIX

Week Two is a massive come-down week. The highs and lows of the first week are a blur, and this is when you and your partner begin to lay the foundations of your routines

5 TIPS FOR NEW MUMS ON HOW TO ENCOURAGE AND SUPPORT THE DAD

1. Show your partner that you respect him as an equal parent and honour his role as a father

2. Support and encourage your partner to grow into his own unique father role, dad style and be a hands-on dad

3. Work with your partner's strengths and acknowledge his efforts

4. Allow your partner to do things differently to you and to not be 'perfect'

5. To ensure there are no concerns and issues between the dad and Mother-in-Law, have a conversation with your partner about the support role your Mum will play and create some clear boundaries

and rhythms as parents. For most dads however, this generally means heading back to work. Now that there's a new bub in the mix and a new role to play, the challenge that presents is to work out how to get the new balance of relationship-fatherhood-work-self-sleep in some kind of harmony; it's a constant process of balancing and re-balancing.

Creating space for fatherhood in this new mix is a massive adjustment. The opportunity that I like to present to new dads is to create some routines and rhythms around work that build upon your first week efforts of being a hands-on dad. For example, morning walks with baby before work, or you taking on the role of giving your baby a night bath when you come home from work (or even better, bath with your baby as skin to skin is wonderful for bonding). Having something that's just for you and baby in your day becomes a special time that you look forward to and brings a sense of deep fulfilment and accomplishment.

Prioritising and fulfilling on the commitment of daily dad time can be both joyous and challenging. The early days are all about parenting moment to moment, trial and error, and being flexible. So don't get too fixated on a plan. What might work one day doesn't guarantee that it will work the next. But if you spend enough time with your child, you'll get to know their cues, their personality, and their rhythms. You'll develop your own strategies for managing challenging moments. There is nothing more empowering as a dad than being alone with your child and knowing with a quiet, strong, masculine confidence that you're capable of thriving!

By cultivating skills, confidence, behaviours, attitudes, beliefs, and habits that are positively rooted in your Father role in the early days, you're laying the foundations of a rewarding Fatherhood journey, relationship and family life.

Darren is passionate about being an active and engaged Dad / Step Dad to his 3 kids. He is a facilitator of Building Better Dads, an education and mentoring course for expectant fathers at the Men & Family Centre in Lismore NSW, and has just joined the team of presenters at Beer & Bubs: childbirth education for dads at the pub.

They Start Out Natural. Let's Keep it That Way'

Increasingly, as we become aware of how chemicals can harmfully affect ourselves and the environment, we begin to search for organic products.

At Little Innoscents our products are healthier for your baby – there are no synthetically active ingredients, no mineral oils, no paraben preservatives, no synthetic colours or fragrances, no harsh detergents or surfactants that can be very harmful to your hair and skin. Our skincare range is formulated using only the finest natural oils, butters, plant extracts and active ingredients available. They are an ideal alternative to help relieve and soothe many sensitive skin complaints.

- No 1. Selling Certified Organic baby brand
- Brand Established over 5 years

Order online for FREE shipping
www.littleinnoscents.com.au

CERTIFIED ORGANIC BABY SKINCARE

Placenta Encapsulation
The revival of an ancient medicine that's nurturing new mothers

Some celebrity mums are doing it, some homebirthing mums are doing it, some scheduled caesarean birthing mums are doing it ... **Kristin Beckedahl** *explains why women are holding onto their placentas, just as tightly as their newborns*

For many new Mums 'life after baby' tends to hit home around Day 3 postpartum. It is also well known as Day 1 of the common 'baby blues' period. Its usually on this day when all the gloriously high levels of hormones like oestrogen and progesterone that were surging through a woman's pregnant body, dramatically drop like a free fall at the end of a roller coaster. This descent back to preconception levels is also marked by the arrival of her milk supply; which has its own set of unfamiliar and at times, uncomfortable sensations! The combination of this, plus the adjustment to life with a new family member can leave a woman feeling quite emotional, teary, overwhelmed, anxious, exhausted and downright all-over-the-shop!

This common 'baby blues' period affects between 50 - 80% of women, beginning around Day 3 - 4 postpartum and extending into the second week of early motherhood. Postnatal depression (PND) on the other hand, affects 10 - 15% of first-time mothers in Australia. Interestingly, the average onset for PND is about 2 months, and most women seek help or treatment around the 4 month mark. The hormonal changes after having a baby are recognised as a strong contributing factor to the incidence of baby blues, and to PND.

But what if there was a natural way to ease this hormonal let-down and support the transition into the postpartum for new mothers? Enter, placentophagy. The consumption of the placenta is a ritual that dates back to ancient Egypt, and it has been practiced for thousands of years in Traditional Chinese Medicine (TCM). It is popular in Europe, although its a relatively new concept to the western world, and still in its infancy in Australia.

We know that 99 percent of all mammals ingest their own placentas immediately after the birth, so maybe it's we humans that are missing the boat. Volumes of research reveal that throughout pregnancy, this incredible, temporary endocrine organ of life produces progesterone, oestrogen, prolactin, oxytocin and relaxin, iron, and Vitamin B6, just to name a few! We also know that as much as 33% of the placenta by weight, is iron. Good to know considering a woman can lose up to 18% of her iron stores after giving birth.

The theory behind the practice is simple; ingesting the placenta (that once created the nutrients and hormones that were lost during birth) helps the physiological descent back to pre-conception levels, a lot smoother and certainly kinder, on the new mother.

Although a compelling and fascinating topic, there have been limited human research studies performed. Of the studies that have been done, researchers have drawn strong correlations to the components of the placenta, and the physiological effects to the new mother during the postpartum*:
- Decreasing the likelihood of developing the 'baby blues' and/or postnatal depression
- Increasing breast milk production and let-down reflex
- Decreasing the incidence of iron deficiency and/or iron deficiency anaemia
- Minimising postnatal bleeding; helping the uterus return to its pre-pregnancy state
- Reducing stress levels; leaving mothers feeling calmer
- Increasing energy levels; helping mothers cope with the needs of a new baby

So, how does the placenta contribute so greatly? It is all due to the bio-specific hormones and chemicals contained within the placenta:
1. Gonadotrophin - this is the precursor to oestrogen, progesterone and testosterone
2. Prolactin - the hormone involved in stimulating milk production
3. Oxytocin - the hormone of bonding; produced during breastfeeding to promote maternal bonding between mother and baby. Also helps uterus to return to prepregnancy size, therefore reducing postpartum bleeding.

> *'Ingesting the placenta (that once created the nutrients and hormones that were lost during birth) helps the physiological descent back to pre-conception levels, a lot smoother and certainly kinder, on the new mother.'*

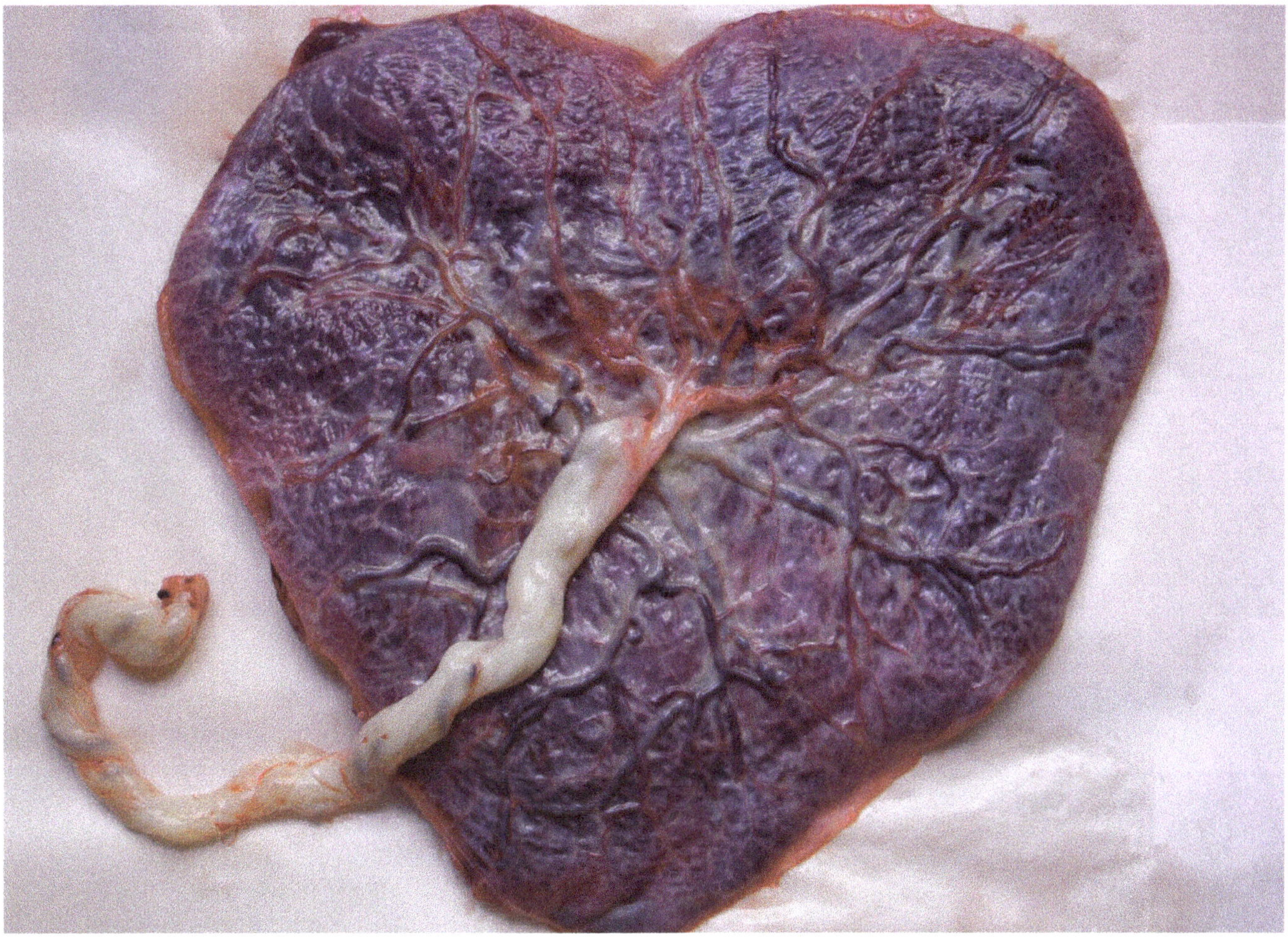

4. Interferon and Gammaglobulin - both stimulate the immune system to protect against infection
5. Thyroid Stimulating Hormone - boosts and balances metabolism and energy levels
6. Cortisone - combats stress and unlocks energy stores in body
7. Prostaglandins - anti-inflammatory hormones
8. Haemoglobin - helps replenishe iron, reducing postnatal iron deficiency and/or anaemia, and the potential, subsequent postnatal depression symptoms
9. Urokinase Inhibiting Factor & Factor XIII - helps reduce bleeding and enhances wound healing

For those whom know very little about placentophagy, its a tough concept to swallow (pun intended). There certainly

Placenta Capsules-
"an idea that's easy to swallow".

Placenta Encapsulation
MELBOURNE • ADELAIDE
• **Placenta Care and Service**
Certificate 4 in Contribute to OHS Processes
Certificate 2 in Food Safety Procedures

motheringthemother™

• **Doula Service**
• **Childbirth Education and Preparation**

Call 0425 775 406
E: tammydoula@gmail.com
www.motheringthemother.com.au

Confident Birth & Wellbeing

Natural therapies for birth & beyond
Childbirth education, Labour support, Placenta processing

Vickie Hingston-Jones
Childbirth Educator, Doula, Complementary Therapist
e: vickie@confidentbirth.com.au
p: (02) 6294 0069 m: 0422 008 759
w: confidentbirth.com.au

The Original The Best

PBi

Placenta Encapsulation Specialist Training Course

Become the Expert in YOUR Community!

Latest Placentophagy Research
5 Modules of evidence-based research
Placenta Preparation Instructions
Training Manual and DVD
Continuing Education modules
Pay-as-you-go option
Meets safety standards in:
  * Australia, Canada, UK & USA
✿ Online and self-paced

Discounts for AU Specialists!

Visit
PlacentaCourse.com/AU
for details & offers

---

are misconceptions about the practice, just trawl the internet and you'll find instructions for smoothies, broths, soups, stews or the frozen 'raw' pills. Amongst these you will also find the (somehow) more socially acceptable, and for many, more convenient practice of placenta encapsulation.

HOW IS IT DONE?

The process should begin ideally within the first 4 - 24 hours after the birth. The placenta, which should have been refrigerated as soon as possible after the birth, is gently rinsed of any blood or clots, and the membranes and cord are removed. It is then slowly and lightly steamed. Some use traditional herbs here, either within the steaming water or with the placenta. It is then sliced thinly, placed into a dehydrator for many hours until it becomes quite brittle. The pieces are then ground (resembling the consistency of fine sea salt) and then encapsulated into average sized clear capsules.

The average sized placenta, from an averaged size baby yields about 140 - 160 capsules, although some placentas make well over 200. They look and taste like any other vitamin or herbal capsule. Due to the TCM method of preparing the placenta, it becomes a preserved product and when stored correctly (refrigerator initially, then freezer) it can be kept indefinitely.

Women are instructed to take the capsules anywhere from once to three times daily.

The dosing is always higher in the initial period (i.e the first week) then begins to decline as the weeks progress through the postpartum. After this time, most women will have ample leftover so can keep them to use at a later time. This can be any stressful, or hormonally transitional time e.g. the return of her menstrual cycle, heading back to work, needing to express regularly or weaning from breastfeeding.

Premature, 'over-due' or twin babies placentas can also be used. If an induction or epidural (or other narcotic drugs) were used in labour and/or a caesarean birth occurred, the placenta can still be used. This is because it does not 'store' these compounds as such; they are sent back to the mother's liver to be detoxified from her system. Some of these drugs also have a very short half-life in the body (meaning how long it takes for half of it to be eliminated from the bloodstream). It is difficult to know whether such drugs have an affect on the capsules, since there are no studies to show the safety or efficacy of ingesting placentas that have been exposed to drugs in labour. However anecdotally, such drugs as syntocinon and those used with an epidural, do not seem to cause ill effects for mothers who ingest their own placenta capsules.

Placentas birthed in water are also fine. If the mother tested positive for Group B Strep before or during labour, the placenta can still be used as the steaming kills off this bacteria. Placentas with light meconium staining or showing signs of calcification, can also be prepared for encapsulation, after a few extra steps in the process. Even if the placenta was frozen soon after the birth, it can be encapsulated after defrosting.

It would seem nothing can mimic the abundance of constituents found within this lifegiving organ. Capturing the essence of this wondrous vessel of life, and having it continue to nurture and rebalance the new mother, is perhaps, something our culture needs to rediscover. If using the placenta can help one mother feel significantly better in those early weeks, or to help avoid the baby blues, and prevent the descent into postnatal depression, then the benefits for the whole family speak for themselves.

Blooming
IN ADELAIDE

BUMP ✿ BIRTH
BREASTFEEDING ✿ BABYCARE

0414 701 412
www.bloominginadelaide.com.au

Lactation Consultations, Doula and Placental Encapsulation Services

Support, guidance and encouragement from

'Bump to Birth and Beyond'

By caring experts in the field

Kristin Beckedahl is Naturopath, Nutritionist, Childbirth Educator, Doula and mother of two. Her practice BodyWise BirthWise, focuses on naturopathy support for women's health, fertility, preconception, pregnancy and postnatal health. For more information, please visit www.bodywisebirthwise.com.au

* References:

Hormonal Changes in the Postpartum and Implications for Postpartum Depression, Hendrick et al. (1998); Psychosomatics; 39 (2): 93 -101 Placenta as Lactagagon,

Soykova-Pachnerova E, et al.(1954) *Gynaecologia* 138(6):617-627

Effects of placentophagy on serum prolactin and progesterone concentrations in rats after parturition or superovulation. Blank MS, Friesen HG.(1980); J Reprod Fertil. Nov;60(2):273-8.

Maternal Iron Deficiency Anemia Affects Postpartum Emotions and Cognition, John L. Beard, et al. (2005); J. Nutr. 135: 267–272.

The Impact of Fatigue on the Development of Postpartum Depression, Elizabeth J. Corwin, et.al. (2005); Journal of Obstetric, Gynecologic, & Neonatal Nursing 34 (5), 577–586

Have we forgotten the significance of postpartum iron deficiency? Lisa M. Bodnar, et.al. (2005); American Journal of Obstetrics and Gynecology, 193, 36–44

Iron supplementation for unexplained fatigue in non-anaemic women: double blind randomised placebo controlled trial, F Verdon, et al.(2003); BMJ; 326:1124 (24 May), doi:10.1136/bmj.326.7399.1124

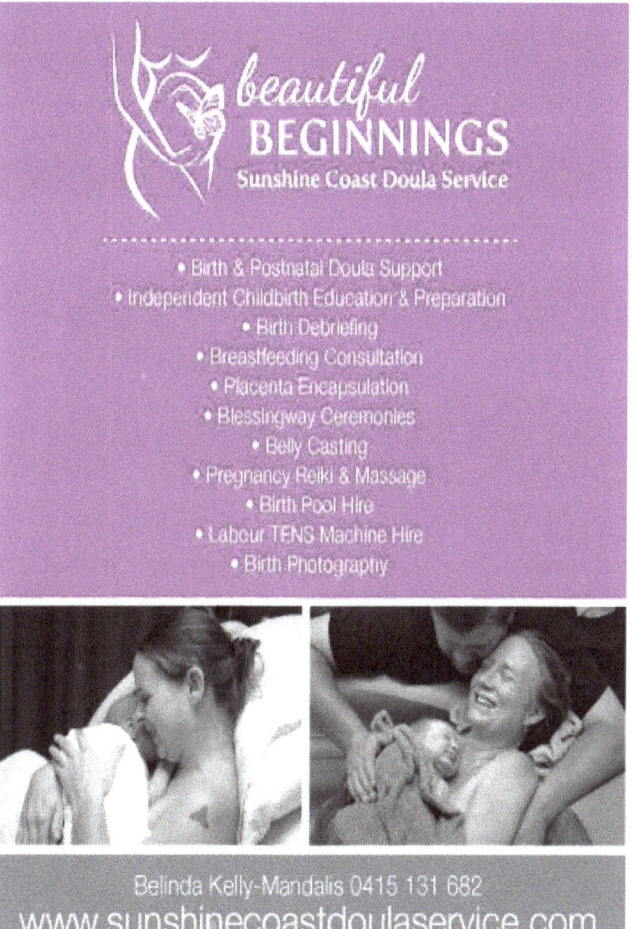

Your Story

Melissa Tuffley tells how her intentions of raising her child (cot, pram, schedules) all became obsolete once she had her baby and followed her instincts.

When I entered the realms of motherhood I had no idea how different the mother I thought I would be was to the mother I have become. I envisioned giving bub a bottle, feeding and sleeping to a set schedule, bub sleeping through by eight weeks in his cot in his bedroom and pushing my pram around with my cooing baby sucking his dummy…hmm how things changed!

I wasn't sure I'd ever breastfeed. I'd not given it much thought and to be honest, the thought wasn't very appealing to me. Then Jack was born. Within minutes he nestled into my chest and from that moment on our breastfeeding relationship was born. No-one warned me that I would have the sorest nipples in the world, or the painful engorgement or, most importantly, the excitement and thrill I would feel when he finally starting latching properly. I'll be honest; I had nights, usually around the 2am mark where I thought "what am I doing?" and maybe just giving him a bottle would be easier. However with another close friend also experiencing the trials and tribulations of a breastfeeding newborn; the support of my husband and lots and lots of newfound research on the topic, I continued. To this day, fifteen months on, pregnant and working, against all odds, we still have a very close and continually flourishing breastfeeding relationship.

Another thing I thought I'd never do, and I mean ever, was co-sleep. It wasn't even an option that entered my mind. I thought it was unsafe and didn't want to "create a rod for my own back" by having bub in bed with us; my sleep was too important etc etc. Fast forward eight weeks after the birth of Jack and co-sleeping, actually bed sharing, was the norm in our household. I honestly do not know how we would have got through without it and after reading so much research on the subject now, I am so glad we did! The funny thing is we came to love bub coming into our bed, snuggling up for a breastfeed then falling asleep soundly beside us. When he'd stir I'd put him back to sleep and we'd all wake up together in the morning. It was absolute bliss. Then suddenly at thirteen months he just decided he didn't want to sleep in our bed anymore. He wanted to sleep alone and went from waking a minimum of three times a night to sleeping through! I was definitely a bit sad that he decided to jump the parent ship and sleep solo … I never saw it coming and I do miss many aspects of co-sleeping! Maybe that will change again down the line!

Babywearing…what is that?? Before Jack I thought other than carrying him in my arms that prams were the only mode of baby transport. For some reason though I just wanted him close to me and that suited him as he never wanted to be put down! So I started researching babywearing. I ordered a Hug a Bub and Manduca online, they arrived in the mail and quickly became my lifesavers. I would take the Hug a Bub everywhere. As soon as Jack became restless or sleepy in he went and was settled and asleep within minutes. I did all my shopping, groceries, walking the dogs and even lunch dates with Jack asleep in his carrier. Also, Jack had quite severe reflux until he was about six months so sleeping upright on me was sometimes the only option. My husband loved carrying him as well, Jack

Another thing I thought I'd never do, and I mean ever, was co-sleep … I thought it was unsafe' and didn't want to 'create a rod for my own back'

sleeping on his chest was a wonderful bonding experience for them both! Again, at about eleven months he decided he didn't want to go in the carrier anymore and unfortunately we haven't used it since. But I have wonderful memories of carrying him close to my heart. He still insists on being carried everywhere, just on my hip these days!

Scheduling… This was so enticing to me. Living by a schedule, knowing when bub would sleep and eat and for how long. In the beginning I tried, oh how I tried to stick to one of these schedules. I thought I was failing as a parent because Jack just didn't read the same books and wasn't interested in what he was "supposed" to be doing. I can't remember at what point I gave up, but when I did, it was such a relief, for both of us! I started feeding him when he was hungry and putting him down when he showed tired signs. This was a breakthrough for us and I felt so much more relaxed when we just went with the flow.

Crying it out. Hmm, this became a contentious topic of conversation. Jack wouldn't sleep in his cot. He flat out refused for a long time. Hence we started baby wearing and co-sleeping. He was happy and content when he was with me. I did feel pressure to leave him in his bed to cry it out. We were told he was manipulating us and that every time we picked him up he was winning. Thankfully my husband felt the same instinctive nurturing desire to love and protect our son and we agreed that no matter what we wouldn't let him cry it out. I admit it was hard some nights when I was so tired I felt physically ill, but the alternative was worse. I truly believe from the bottom of my heart that a baby cries out to you because he is tired, scared, hungry or lonely. He needs comfort. He needs his mother or father. He isn't trying to beat you or trick you; he just wants to be with you. Sure crying it out "works" if you consider your child giving up on you to comfort him "working". We never wanted our beautiful son to give up on us. As soon as he awoke and started crying we would comfort him. Now at 15 months he happily goes to sleep in his bed, he never cries and he is a very happy, secure and confident child. I am so grateful that my husband and I never listened to the cry it out supporters but rather comforted and loved our son; even through all those long trying nights!

There are so many other learning experiences I could share. Motherhood has changed me completely. The love I feel for my child is indescribable and no-one could have prepared me for the overwhelming instinct to protect, love and nurture this little human being that catapulted himself into our lives. Every day is amazing with him. It is the most challenging yet rewarding experience of my life. Overall; the biggest thing I have learned is to trust what feels right for Jack and I and to believe in myself. I don't think what I do and how I parent is right, full stop. I do think however that it is right for us; and that is all I wish for every mother and father on this wonderful, tumultuous, learning curve called parenthood.

If you would like to share your natural parenting story with other natural parents, simply e-mail it to editor@nurtureparentingmagazine.com.au Each published letter will also receive three books from Pick-a-Woo-Woo Books valued at $44.85.

100% organic cotton

unique
sustainable
safe

ensuring your child takes each step in style

growing footprints

growingfootprints.com.au
sales@growingfootprints.com.au

1. Rose Print Bodysuit 2. Dusty Blue Babygro
3. Rose Print Gathered Dress 4. Navy Spot Shirred Dress

Unschooling:
Inspired Thinking or Educational Neglect?

Many parents would not hesitate to tell people how the school system does not cater for their specific child. What if there was a way that your child could engage in self-directed learning? **Chaley-Ann Scott** *discusses 'unschooling' as an alternative to conventional schooling*

It's 11:00 a.m. on a school day. My ten-year-old son and eleven-year old daughter have only been up for an hour and are respectively playing with Legos and making a necklace. They are focused and happy and I am trying not to interfere—because in our house this is education. For Jack and Molly, there is no early rising, no one telling them what to do, and no restrictions—just freedom to play and follow their interests, whilst I provide support and resources if required. It's every child's dream. Welcome to the world of "unschooling," an approach to education that lets children decide what, when and how they will learn each day.

Unschooling is a popular method of homeschooling, a legal and fast-growing trend in many countries in the world including the USA, Australia, Canada, New Zealand and the UK. In the US, over 1.5 million children were registered as homeschooled in 2007, reflecting a 74 per cent increase in eight years.

Parents cite numerous reasons for choosing to homeschool their children—from the wish to avoid bullying at school to the desire to prioritise instruction in the family's religious beliefs. My reasons for choosing this path were reactionary—Molly had a huge thirst for knowledge but after a year of school that was all but gone. She was miserable. So in desperation we pulled her out of school and began our journey from homeschooling into unschooling.

Like us, many homeschoolers start off following a curriculum, but most end up following, at least in part, the unschooling philosophy. The term "unschooling" was coined in 1977 by American education reformer John Holt, who believed that parents should not attempt to duplicate conventional schooling in their homes. Therefore, in unschooling there are no mandatory books, no curriculum, no tests and no grades. Unschoolers believe these trappings of traditional education are unnecessary because, as author and unschooling advocate Sandra Dodd explains, "Learning cannot be turned off…Given a rich environment, learning becomes like the air—it's in and around us." It's radical stuff I know. How can a child left to direct their own education possibly knuckle down to hard work and fulfill their potential?

Many traditional homeschoolers believe they can't. Gail Paquette, a homeschooling mother of two and founder of the web site Hometaught.com, is one of unschooling's most vocal critics. "A child-led approach may develop the child's strengths but does nothing to develop his weaknesses and broaden his horizons," she writes. "I [mostly] disagree with the premise that children can teach themselves what they want to learn, when (and if) they want to learn it. Certainly children do learn some things on their own, but their often roundabout way of going at learning is not necessarily the best way."

Unschoolers, however, strongly disagree that children don't learn naturally in the "right" way and therefore need to be shown how to learn. They claim that children really do know best when it comes to their learning, and we should put our trust in them. When children are pushed and cajoled into learning something they aren't interested in or aren't quite ready for, the teacher commonly meets with resistance or stress. Unschooling author John Taylor-Gatto, in his infamous acceptance speech for New York Teacher of the Year said: "It is absurd and anti-life to be part of a system that compels you to listen to a stranger reading poetry when you want to learn to construct buildings, or to sit with a stranger discussing the construction of buildings when you want to read poetry." On the other hand, when children are free to do things they have chosen to do—in their own way, on their own timetables—then the learning thrives. Unschoolers believe that their approach fosters a love of learning, whereas conventional schooling or school-at-home does the exact opposite.

Holt wrote: "All I am saying is … trust children. Nothing could be more simple — or more difficult. Difficult, because to trust children we must trust ourselves — and most of us were taught as children that we could not be trusted." Thirty years later, the belief that children are essentially capable, curious,

'When children are free to do things they have chosen to do - in their own way, on their own timetables - then the learning thrives'

independent and self-disciplined is hard for conventional parents to swallow. With the wealth of parenting manuals on the shelves, we are encouraged that our instincts should make way for structure and planning to be 'successful' parents.

In our house I noticed that when I stopped poking and prodding the kids to do things that looked like learning to me (from my schooled perspective) – bookwork, projects, science experiments etc - then the real learning really took off. I just had to have faith in my children that they were learning all the time – even when it didn't look like it to me. Not surprisingly, the approach is becoming increasingly popular with attachment parents, due to its emphasis on placing trust in children to know what they need and when they need it. The natural extension of trusting that our babies and toddlers know when they are ready to wean, sleep alone, or use the toilet, is trusting that children know what, when, and how they should learn as they grow.

So how do unschoolers learn? For them, learning happens simply while living life, as they engage in activities such as listening to stories, cooking, gardening, doing puzzles, building, doing artwork, experimenting, watching movies, playing video games, having conversations, and using money. When children have an interest in more advanced concepts that their parents don't understand, they can seek outside resources that teach the material, such as books, computer games, DVDs, classes, or tutors. When people ask my children if they do 'school-at-home', with no coaching from me my son has always responded with, 'No, we learn through fun'. It's true, we are learning through fun—all of us, all the time. That's how adults learn, so why not kids? It's hard for people to understand this concept because school teaches us that we aren't there to have fun, but to learn—as if they are completely separate entities.

Sandra Dodd explains, "Learning isn't in fancy books or computer games; it all happens in the ideas children have, in the trivial facts they fit together to come up with their view of the world—past, present, and future. You don't need a lesson or a unit to show a child what's wonderful about woodgrain, ice crystals on the windshield, or birdsongs. Five seconds' worth of pointing and saying, 'Look, these trees were not native to North America' might possibly lead to an hour-long discussion, or a lifelong fascination. Bringing something interesting home, browsing in an antique shop, listening to new music on instruments you've never heard—all those build neural pathways and give you a chance to be together in a special place."

I have been blown away by how much learning comes out of our day-to-day conversations. Over breakfast today we began idly chatting about dinosaurs which organically led (somehow!) to Italian food and then to Islamic fundamentalism! The connections between different subjects is amazing to me, and I can see clearly they are absorbing so much information all the time. I didn't always feel this way however. I had fears and anxiety around learning the basics, particularly when it came to reading, and I am not alone. Dodd says this is a common area of concern amongst parents but, after twenty years of involvement with the unschooling movement, she claims unschooled children always learn to read. "I know of not one single unschooler who didn't learn to read," she says. "I've seen a dozen unschooled kids close-up learn to read...and have accounts of hundreds of others. They read. Some suddenly, some gradually, but every single one of them reads."

My own children can read fluently and had no formal instruction whatsoever. They aren't child geniuses but just normal children. Molly decided she wanted to learn at six years old and would ask to be read to, and would ask me what certain words said, and over a year she eventually just picked it up. My son's journey was more interesting. I will admit it caused me great angst when, by aged eight, he had showed no interest whatsoever in books or reading in general, and I started to panic and question our path. Stories from unschoolers whose children learnt to read late, but still read eventually with no ill effects reassured me a little and I managed to keep my fears away from him. Then one day he started fluently reading a newsbrief off the computer to me. "How did you know what that said?", I asked, gobsmacked, "I dunno. Oh yeah, I forgot to tell you that I can read now," he off-handedly replied. No big deal. I really don't know how he learnt but I think it had to do with computer games. He was motivated to learn how to play more strategically so he started looking at the instruction booklets—he must have been ready and he worked it out by himself almost overnight. No fuss or stress.

I am often asked how my children will cope in the real world that requires qualifications to "succeed"? They can take any test they want to if they require it to reach a further goal, and university is one of many options available to them. There are no separate statistics available on unschoolers at present, but numerous studies have been undertaken on all forms of homeschooling, including unschooling—most notably by an independent agency, the National Home Education Research Institute (NHERI), which has conducted and collected research for two decades. Their findings in 2009 report that the home-educated typically score up to 30 percentile points above public-school students on standardized academic achievement tests, and that they are increasingly being actively recruited by universities.

The NHERI research also supports the view that the home-educated are not in fact the social misfits that many

would expect. "The home-educated are doing well, typically above average, on measures of social, emotional, and psychological development. Research measures include peer interaction, self-concept, leadership skills, family cohesion, participation in community service, and self-esteem," the research reveals. My own children certainly aren't missing out socially – every day they are busy with a club, a sleepover, or a playdate, and mix with both schooled and unschooled children.

A number of adults who were educated this way as children have overwhelmingly positive things to say about their educations. Armed only with open university courses, driving ambition, and Grade 8 harp, Helen Thompson, 18, is studying to be a doctor. "My experience has taught me to follow my passions without restraint." She adds, "University is a shock to everyone, but being unschooled probably helped me settle in more quickly than some people, who felt uncomfortable initially with the change from more directed learning. Every week we attend a tutorial. At the end, we are given a list of 20 books to read for the next week, which you have to get on with. My peers are struggling because they have been taught that learning is a chore—something to endure—whereas I see it as fun. I love to read and increase my knowledge so uni to me is just like unschooling but with tutorials."

Unschooling alumna — now unschooling mum—Vanessa Wilson, 31, testifies, "As a kid the world is full of so much that school cannot give… I credit my education for my insatiable love of learning".

And what of those who don't choose to pursue advanced formal education? "Instead of college," says Tara Wagner, 29, "I chose massage school and self-education for entrepreneurship. To me that is the best thing about [unschooling]: the freedom to create your own life, to heal, to grow unhindered, to explore without imposed limitations. Amazing things happen inside of freedom."

The unschooling philosophy is clearly a complete reversal of the educational wisdom millions of us have accepted and followed for decades about learning. Unschooling will undoubtedly appeal to those parents who are fed up with the micromanagement of their children's lives, because it disregards conventional wisdom about giftedness, age-appropriate learning, and competition. Ironically, though, it appears that despite not being groomed for top university admission, these kids often end up there anyway.

Jane Dobson, 18, struggled through her early school years due to so-called 'learning difficulties'. In desperation, her mother pulled her out of school when she was 10 and started unschooling her, convinced that her daughter didn't have a deficiency at all – just that her learning style wasn't being catered for at school. Free of labels, and given the freedom to pursue her own interests, she discovered she had a big talent for design.

She has now turned her life around from the days when thought she was 'stupid' in school, and has been accepted at QUT university to study Landscape Architecture. Her brother, Steven, 16, has no plans for university, but is working already as a concert pianist, attracting work around the country. These kids know they are smart and are busy carving out careers for themselves. "As we get older, I think things are going to get less complicated and we won't be judged so much," says Steven, "I mean, when you can say 'hey look I am doing great and I am happy', people start thinking well {it} can't be that bad". It seems, in the case for unschooling, the proof is in the pudding.

I feel liberated that I am no longer focused on the destination when it comes to my children, but on the journey, and have faith in them that they will reach their potential in their own way on their own clock. I find it tremendously rewarding, and a real privilege, to spend so much time with my children watching them learn in amazing and unexpected ways. This is why my kids can spend as much time gazing into space as they like. They are currently absorbed in their activities and I wonder what they are thinking – are they in the midst of developing advanced theories? Solving world peace? Considering deep philosophical arguments?

Molly shuffles in her seat and prepares to speak, looks up and says, "Mum - I hate my new jeans."

Chaley-Ann Scott is the author of The Shepherdess; Progressive Mothering Without Control, a parenting counsellor, and mother of four. For more information, visit www.progressiveparenting.org

Beyond Birth

with Julia Jones

Nourishing Traditions: A World of Postpartum

Have you noticed our cultures divorce and postnatal depression rates and wondered if it has to be this hard? Have you wondered why so many educated and loving parents resort to control crying? Maybe you've questioned how the human race has survived this long if breastfeeding really is as difficult as it seems to be in modern times?

The word doula was first coined by anthropologist Dana Raphael to describe a woman who came to be with the mother after childbirth, the concept of a birth doula came many years later. Raphael found this pattern of mothering the new mother with very specific rituals and customs occurring in 178 different cultures.

There are many striking similarities amongst postpartum traditions. The two most common are the use of heat through therapies, food and environment and the idea of confinement for a specific period of time, usually 30-40 days. The vast majority of these cultures also include strict dietary guidelines, oil and herbal treatments, massage, belly wrapping, limited bathing and restrictions on visitors.

By contrast in our modern world we discharge women from hospital as early as four hours after birth, with men lucky to have two weeks off paid work to support their partners. We often live away from our extended family. When modern women are pregnant they are showered with attention, but once the baby is born Korean born American nurse Yeoun Soo Kim-Godwin points out there always seems to be someone more important than our mothers.

"The message conveyed to American women is that the role of the woman is less important than that of the physician during giving birth. Gifts and celebrations are centered around the newborn rather than the mother (e.g. baby showers, christenings, visits from friends and relatives to see the baby)"

It's no surprise then that the way we neglect our mothers is reflected in all sorts of outcomes including, most obviously, breastfeeding rates. In her research that led to the modern concept of a doula, Dana Raphael made a profound revelation:

"I had discovered that there was a physiological process (breastfeeding) that needed to have something in place in the culture or else the lactation function would not work. I don't know of any other biological process that needs the culture to supply support… if you don't have that support, usually you cannot feed your baby."

What mothers in our culture may consider a luxury, most traditional cultures would consider essential. My teacher, a very wise woman named Ysha Oakes, taught me the phrase '40 days for 40 years' to show the significance that these 40 days of rejuvenation have on the rest of a womans life. The sacred window after birth is an opportunity to heal even chronic or lifelong conditions permanently, or on the other hand, if women are neglected during this 'golden month' they can develop long term emotional, mental or physical health problems.

If you want to enjoy your baby and feel supported, confident, healthy and loved, you may like to invite a postnatal doula into your home to nurture you whilst you nurture your new baby.

Julia works with pregnant women and new mums who want to avoid feeling exhausted and overwhelmed. She is an Ayurvedic postnatal doula and founder of Newborn Mothers in Perth, Western Australia

Tantrums: Evaporate or Nurture?

Every parent starts to get a little stressed when they know a tantrum is coming ~ especially if it is out in public. However, tantrums are not necessarily a 'bad' thing. **Naomi Aldort** *explains when a tantrum should be nurtured and when a tantrum should be evaporated.*

Little Lee came into the kitchen and asked his mother for a dessert. His mother said, "If you want something sweet, there are cherries, grapes or dried fruit." "I want only watermelon, that's what I want. Nothing else." said the boy.

I was sitting close by and saw the tantrum building up. Lee stamped his foot lightly, he frowned and his voice became tight as he was repeating his plea and was ready to explode. (The real need here was not the watermelon but a need for connection and recognition.) At that moment I said, "There is no watermelon and you want to have some! You are getting yourself into a tantrum. Let's have a tantrum about it together; a double tantrum, you and I." The boy smiled and immediately relaxed. I then added, "A triple tantrum, with Mum too," and seeing his Dad walking by, "no, a quadruple tantrum, with Dad too." Lee turned around laughing and looking at his Dad.

Dad acted a slow walk, sneaking out of the room trying to escape. The boy went after him. Dad came back and produced an impressive tantrum, "I want watermelon," he screamed theatrically as he stamped and jumped with a thump. Lee was so excited. He laughed and ran to tell his brother all about it. In a minute we heard the boys playing happily.

We can disarm the buildup of tension simply by telling the truth with humor and playfulness as long as we don't dramatise and are sensitive and tuned into the child's response; we want to avoid patronizing. All I did in this story is call the "white elephant" by her name and gave it complete permission to exist, "Let's have a tantrum."

My validation had no intention that the child would forget about his wish or that the tantrum would vanish. This is just what happened. If I sensed any resistance, I would have changed my words in response the child's emotional state. And, if he had the full tantrum, aware of our understanding, it would have been a healing tantrum. It would have lost the false intention to materialize a watermelon, and instead would have been an honest emotional release.

'in reality, tantrums are the outcome of what we teach our children and are not at all inevitable'

SELF-EXPRESSION OR AN UNCONSCIOUS STRATEGY?

Tantrums have been addressed in many ways, from panic and attempt to stop them, to punishing, yelling, indulging in sympathy or giving the child his wish. Yet, in reality, tantrums are the outcomes of what we teach our children and are not at all inevitable. Yes, children can grow up with very minimal tantrums or even with none at all.

We teach little ones to have tantrums in two ways:

1) By having tantrums ourselves

We demonstrate tantrums when things don't go our way; when the rice burns, the milk spills, we have a flat tire, we are late, and when our own children don't live up to our expectations at bedtime, with friends, siblings, with food etc. The child watches and learns: If things don't go smoothly, its "the end of the world" and "must be fixed."

2) By responding to their upsets and wants with too much drama.

We also teach by the way we respond to the baby and child's requests. Infants and babies start with 100% primal needs that should be responded to fully. However, as they grow, we introduce to them many wants and desires that are not really needs and not always good for them or available. We teach them to seek excitement beyond the magic of the ordinary. And, we often treat these extras as though they were primal needs. With loving intentions, we panic, we compensate, and we give the message, "You cannot handle not getting what you want." This is how they learn to rage; nothing to feel guilty about as you too are learning and doing the best you can.

If your toddler cries when you leave – don't leave; loving and secure connection, are primal needs. However, if your toddler screams for an unhealthy lollie, validate her feelings and get out of the store. And, out of kindness, avoid taking little junior to places that offer things he cannot have. It is too hard for him and he cannot really grasp why you deny him the joy.

NURTURE A HEALING TANTRUM

A tantrum over an unavoidable pain

is a healthy emotional expression. In such a case, an intense crying is the actual need – not to be stopped but nurtured. If a child experiences injury or another calamity, she should cry or rage with your loving listening, presence and (if wanted) embrace.

The child needs to unleash emotions and to know that she has the strength to go through them. Your state of peace tells her that she can handle the intense emotions. It is crucial to avoid showing any desire that her tantrum should cease. Unconditional love means loving her also when she cries and hurts and being the compassionate listener for as long as she needs.

HOW TO SUPPORT EMOTIONAL EXPRESSION

When a toddler or child is authentically upset and we truly cannot provide for his wish, validation and recognition is helpful. It will not stop the tantrum, but allow it to "flourish" so the child can feel healed and be able to move on.

It is crucial not to be the cause of your child's tantrum as much as possible. A child whose life flow is a "yes" to his intent can stay calm in the face of an occasional blow to the flow. Experiencing you on her side, she is more likely to cooperate. Even when her wish is thwarted, you can say "yes" to her intent as in the following example:

In a phone session, a father told me about his daughter who refused to leave the swimming pool when it was closing. Wisely, he asked one of the lifeguards to inform his daughter of the need to leave. This way, she was not angry with her own father so he could be the one supporting her emotional storm. He acknowledged the truth, "I understand," he said to his child, "You wanted to keep swimming." The tantrum intensified and she sobbed in his arms, feeling understood and loved. When she was done, she was peaceful and ready to go home as if nothing happened. That's the magic of full self-expression.

DISARMING THE NEED FOR STRATEGIC TANTRUMS

In a family intensive in my home, a six-year-old girl explained her strategy candidly. She was protesting the delay of going to the playground, screaming and pulling on her mum's shirt. When I asked her, "Xiani, why are you doing this?" She stopped, and with a straight face said, "So mummy will do what I want."

To change a pattern of strategic tantrums, make sure to say "yes" more often and flow with your child's life so she is not constantly frustrated. And, on the other side, when something is not possible, avoid compensating or changing reality in an attempt to stop the tantrum. With such clarity, she will learn that tantrums are not a tool for getting something, but are their own emotional release. A strategic tantrum can vanish before it starts if we recognise it and connect honestly.

For any tantrum, if we provide our loving ear and allow the crying to take place, the child who needs to cry will cry, and the child who is attempting reality change will stop.

WHEN ALLOWING THE CRYING THE TANTRUM EVAPORATES

One night, in our family bed, our youngest (then, a toddler) wanted to be by his brother. But, he kicked and disturbed. His brother kept asking him to stop. At last the older boy asked me to put the little one back on my other side which I did. The toddler protested loudly. I said to him, "I see that you need to cry now and I will hold you so you can cry as long as you need to and then we will go to sleep." Realizing and knowing from experience that I mean it, and that crying is not a tool for anything, he stopped on the spot.

NOTHING BUT EYE CONTACT

At another family intensive retreat at our home, a little girl stood by her mum asking for something mum could not provide in the moment. The girl's body tightened. Her knees locked. She wrinkled her forehead and the tantrum was just about to take off when I made a neutral eye contact with her. (She knew me well and we had a good connection. She stopped and smiled at me. The tantrum evaporated. Again, if she needed to cry, she would have. Her tantrum was not self-expression but a strategy. If she has learned from past experiences that tantrums change outcome, my presence helped her see herself and she was able to drop it and move on and even to laugh at herself.

Make peace with crying, but do not cause it unnecessarily. Or, catch yourself pretending not to notice that an emotional volcano is about to erupt. Kindly acknowledge the truth and show understanding. You will be amazed to discover that "white elephants" are rather friendly.

Naomi Aldort is the author of Raising Our Children, Raising Ourselves and Struggle to Freedom, Power and Joy. Naomi is also an internationally renowned parenting advice columnist, author and public speaker. More information on Naomi is found at www.authenticparent.com

---

pikapú

Modern Cloth Nappies

SAVE. REDUCE. REUSE.

- Newborn to toddler (3-18kg).
- Re-useable, Adjustable.
- Comfortable, Affordable.
- Many gorgeous colours.
- ONE OFF COST FOR YOU!
- Visit our online stores -

Approved By Mums... Used By Dads

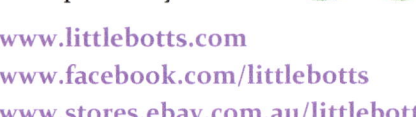

Simple. Clever. Effective.

- Six absorbent layers.
- Easy wash fabrics.
- Quick drying.
- So soft on little botts.
- Simple & easy to use.

www.littlebotts.com
www.facebook.com/littlebotts
www.stores.ebay.com.au/littlebotts

FREE DELIVERY
apply Coupon Code
NURTURE
valid to 31st December 2012
(not valid with any other offer)

Practical Products for Pregnancy, Babies & Toddlers

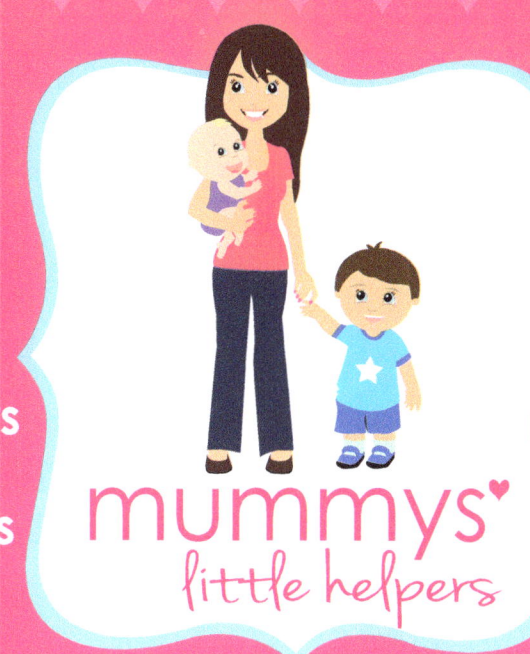

 Find us on Facebook.

100% Organic Cotton

Brolly Sheets

BPA FREE

BPA FREE

BPA FREE

BPA FREE

Mummys' Little Helpers is a retail on-line store run by mums for mums. All of our products are personally tried and tested and are designed to make mums' lives easier. From the wonderful Kala's Magic No Spill Cups to the time-saving Brolly Sheets, we are sure to have something that will help every mum with little ones

www.mummyslittlehelpers.com.au

Children & Trauma What Helps?

*In Part 1 of this two part series on Children and Trauma, **Petrea King** explores what happens for children when they are confronted with trauma and how we can support and assist them to grow through the experience in positive ways*

As parents, we want to protect our children from any trauma whether it is happening in our personal or family lives or in the larger world around us. It is hard to see people we love suffering and that is particularly so when we witness it in our children.

It is easy to think that children are oblivious to trauma as they often have the capacity for laughter, fun and games in the midst of difficult and painful situations. This is not so much a denial of the trauma as a way that children cope with heightened feelings which may feel new, confusing or overwhelming.

Children take on the enormity of what has happened in their own world or in the larger global world and their needs are important to address. Avoid the trap of thinking that children are oblivious to suffering. They may not have a language to express how they're feeling but they are acutely aware of the emotional environment around them and are constantly reading the subtle and not so subtle, signs of stress on adult's faces, in their voices, their postures and their attitudes.

DEALING WITH YOUR EMOTIONS

It can be very challenging to deal with upset feelings in our children when we are feeling disconnected from our usual supports or overwhelmed with our own feelings. Children are very sensitive to the atmosphere around them and to the feelings that the adults are experiencing. If adults are overwhelmed, despairing, anxious or fearful, children find this very upsetting as they look to the adults for reassurance and stability.

You may need to keep the full force of your own grief or emotion for a time when young children are not present. It can be quite frightening for a child to feel that they have lost you to the emotion of the moment along with whatever else has upset them. This is not to say that crying with or in front of our children is a bad thing. On the contrary, it can be very helpful to children to see the healthy expression of feelings of upset. We can demonstrate to them that it is good to cry when you feel upset or are hurt. We can comfort and support each other through our tears and then move onto to dealing with the next thing. We don't want to teach our children that, no matter how bad things might be or how upset we might feel, we must not cry. If we do this, we teach our children to be afraid of tears when really, crying is a natural and healthy way to discharge the upset we feel and can be a blessed relief! Remember, it's hard to kiss someone who's keeping a stiff upper lip!

GRIEF: WHAT TO LOOK FOR

Children enjoy routine and regularity and when this is disrupted due to a natural disaster or some other upset or trauma in their life they lose their usual reference points. These could include disruptions to their daily routines, their contact with friends, family or pets. Profound changes in the physical environment due to flood, cyclone or fire bring their own deep sense of disorientation, loss and upset.

Many children don't possess the emotional literacy to be able to describe or express the feelings that they are experiencing. They may be experiencing new feelings that can be quite disturbing or overwhelming to them and it is good to give them some strategies for naming and expressing what they might be feeling. These feelings may show up through disturbed sleeping or eating patterns, a child becoming shy and reclusive or the opposite, demonstrating angry and boisterous behaviours. Children may revert to previous behaviours that they had already grown through including sucking thumbs, disruptions in toilet training, picky food behaviours, becoming more clingy or experiencing separation anxiety and temper tantrums. These are all signs that the child is struggling to adjust to a changed environment and circumstances.

CULTIVATING COMPASSION

It is important to cultivate compassion in our children. If we ignore or deny another person's pain, even if they are a stranger to us, we miss an opportunity to feel good ourselves. That may sound a strange paradox yet compassion is a complex but positive

> *'Many children don't possess the emotional literacy to be able to describe or express the feelings that they are experiencing'*

emotion and when we feel it, our well-being is improved. It is normal and healthy for children to care about others.

When we feel compassion, it fires our vagus nerve fibres which, in turn helps us to feel calm by slowing our heart rate, lowering our blood pressure and improving our immune system. Sharing another person's suffering can make us healthier if we cultivate compassion in ourselves and our children. When children's compassion is sparked, it is a good idea to harness that feeling in a positive way by involving the child in some activity that channels their concern. That could be in the form of writing a letter or making a drawing depending on the age of the child and the kind of trauma. It could also be useful to get children to make something to send to a more distant disaster or to raise funds to be of assistance. This helps children to feel involved and capable of meeting the challenge of suffering whenever and wherever they encounter it.

Compassion stimulates a desire to ease the suffering of others. It is important to not just allow children to feel sad, upset or compassion for the person, animal or situation, but to then harness and utilise that feeling by doing something that is positive and supportive. This teaches an acceptance of feelings that are painful or distressing and provides the child with a proactive way of soothing themselves by contributing to the happiness of others through helping. In this way we help a child move beyond feeling helpless and powerless to ease someone's suffering to feeling that they have just made a positive contribution to that person's, (or animal's) happiness.

INFORM CHILDREN

Children are fabulous at overhearing conversations but very poor at interpreting what it is they have heard because they have a limited framework and a lack of experience to draw upon. They are very sensitive to people changing or stopping the conversation when they walk into the room. Be mindful if you are talking on the telephone that little ears are straining to catch your emphasis, hesitation or the snippets they hear and could be quite frightened by the tone of fear, anger or frustration in your voice.

Children need to be informed, according to their understanding, about what has happened and what is being done about what has happened. They don't need to know what might happen in the future, what could happen or what is happening in other parts of the world. If there is a traumatic event going on, whether within our own family or in our community, be mindful of protecting children from other traumas that might be happening in the larger world over which they have no control. Children

Discover the #1 Secret to Your Baby Sleeping Peacefully and Easily at

insyncwithinfants.com

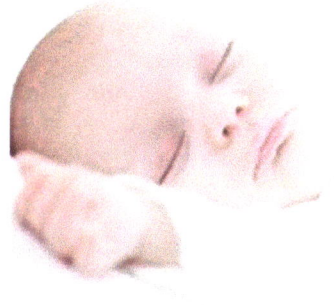

with Leisa ~ RN, Midwife, Child Health Nurse, and Lactation Consultant

1800 880 993

cope far more effectively with the tumult of feelings they might be experiencing if they are given specific tasks and routines and, at the same time are protected from external traumas that don't impact upon them directly. Avoid upsetting conversations in front of children that focus on potential future scenarios that may or may not happen or disasters that are happening globally.

Limit the amount of time that children are exposed to television reports and images of destruction or devastation. It is very difficult for children to witness suffering over which they have no control and they can't see what is being done to ease the anguish on the faces of people on the television. We don't want our children to become oblivious to the suffering of others because upsetting images are constantly playing on a television screen in their home.

EMBRACE THEIR FEELINGS

Let children know that it is normal and healthy to feel upset, worried, sad, frightened, angry, or whatever the feeling might be that they are experiencing. Help them to name the feeling if possible. Ask them where they feel that feeling in their body or explain to them where you feel feelings in your body. You can talk about how your heart hurts when you feel sad, or how your chest tightens or your heart races when you feel overwhelmed, or how your tummy turns when you think of what needs to be done to get things right again or how your head feels like it's going to burst if you feel angry and upset about what has happened.

Children need to know that it is fine to feel anything. It is what we do with our feelings, which is important. We don't want to hurt ourselves, other people or property because of how we feel. Indeed, it's good to have an agreement with children that no matter how strongly we might be feeling something, it is never OK to hurt yourself, someone else or to damage property. This can be difficult for many adults who were not given any emotional support, awareness or understanding themselves of how to express their feelings when they were young. Indeed we often want to 'contain' messy emotions in our children if we are scared of those feelings in ourselves.

Sometimes scaling the feeling from 0 – 10 can help children become more skilful in expressing themselves. For instance, they might be feeling sad or sooky and we can ask them, "on a scale of 0 – 10 how sooky are you feeling? Are you just a little bit sooky – say around a 2 or 3 or are you feeling seriously sooky around a 9 or a 10?"

You can do the same with anger, frustration, loneliness or any feeling. By talking about the feeling and scaling it, you can then help the child to learn how to calm or soothe themselves by knowing what action might work with their feelings depending on the intensity. For instance, if a child is feeling a '4' on the grumpy scale, ask them where they are feeling the grumpiness in their body. Is it in their chest? Does their head feel full? Are their muscles tightening up? Perhaps if a child is at a '4' on the grumpy scale, they may be able to calm and soothe themselves by telling themselves to be calm and focusing on their breathing, being aware of the rising and falling of their belly for instance. If however, they are feeling a '10' on the grumpy scale, then it might be useful to know what they can channel that energy into so that they can settle themselves. Do they need to run to the back fence? Would kicking a cardboard box be helpful? Perhaps a punching bag or some other physical exertion that would use up some of the stress chemicals they are experiencing could be helpful.

You can help a child to express their feelings by talking about the feelings that you're having and what you're doing to express them or how you let them go. You might even show children how to breathe deeply to release their feelings by focusing on the rising and falling of their tummy when they breathe, perhaps breathing in sunshine or something that the child will relate to, and then breathing out any feelings they might be experiencing. They can visualise them flowing out of their body as a dark cloud or a particular colour for instance.

For young children you might want to cut out a range of animal photos that express different feelings and ask the child to pick out the picture that looks like how they feel. They can put the animal picture with the feeling written underneath up on the wall with blue tack and this helps the child to see that their feelings come and go and that they don't feel the same way all the time. It also helps them to feel that it is quite normal to have these (perhaps) unfamiliar feelings. Share with your children some of the feelings that you have experienced and let them know what you did to help yourself with that. For instance, "Yesterday I felt really sad about all the things that I have lost. I had a good cry about it and it helped me to realise that while my possessions/house/friends/loved ones have gone, you and I are still here and together we can get through this".

Petrea King is the author of children's books, including You, Me & the Rainbow, Rainbow Kids and The Rainbow Garden, and five books for adults. Petrea is also the Founder and CEO, Quest for Life Foundation www.questforlife.com.au

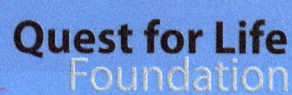

A rainbow is a powerful visual image...

...that helps children feel connected and safe. Petrea's first childrens' book, **You, Me & the Rainbow**, wraps Mariah in a rainbow each night. **Rainbow Kids**, continues the rainbow image taking children on a journey of discovery filled with friendship, compassion and rainbow colours. **The Rainbow Garden**, helps children to see the value in everyone's contribution and how important it is not to judge by appearances.

Rainbow Connection, Petrea's CD for children, has four guided relaxation practices.

*The **Quest for Life Foundation** provides a variety of services to inspire and support people living with the challenges of cancer, chronic illness, loss, grief, trauma, anxiety and depression.*

Petrea King's bestselling books and CDs and rainbow gift items are available through our online shop www.questforlife.com.au/shop.

www.questforlife.com.au
Online shop: 02 4883 6805
Quest for Life Foundation: 1300 941 488

Music for Soothing & Bonding!

Music is a great way for parents to bond with their child. It can also help aid a child's development, or soothe an ill mood reports **Tara Hashambhoy**

Sharing music is a wonderful way to nurture a child/parent bond. Music can be incorporated into any time of day – having a sing-a-long in the car, or quietly listening whilst having a cuddle. Both of these examples can involve turning on the stereo and listening to a favourite CD.

Music (recorded or live) can be a strong positive force for all humans, and therefore you want to find suitable, special music for your children. Many recordings marketed at parents claim to soothe, or facilitate child development, however music marketed as such is not the only music that will give these benefits. To help you make informed choices, here are some guidelines to help you discover wonderful music for the family.

- Like adults, children have different moods and emotions throughout the day. Music can be used to enhance or diffuse emotional states (eg. gentle music may help a child relax or sleep and lively music can be for playtime! Try to include some of each into your collection).
- Children (especially babies) prefer gentle sounds – acoustic folk and classical styles are generally suitable, though you can also find gentle rock/ pop albums that will be appropriate! Children also like a steady beat, even in calm music – a steady beat is soothing and is easy to move to.
- Include a sing-along CD: there are many CDs with traditional songs and nursery rhymes. These are easy to learn and fun to sing together. Music with words encourages language development and appreciation of poetic forms.
- Encourage your child to engage with music through playing instruments, singing and dancing. Keep some instruments and toys handy – instruments can be played whilst scarves and toys are props for creatively interpreting songs or music.
- Good music for children is good music for parents too! Don't choose a CD just because it claims to be good for children - listen and make up your own mind. Remember, you'll likely have to listen to an album or song over and over. Make sure it won't drive you batty! Most online music shops let you preview before you buy.
- Remember: Recorded music is only one way to experience music.

Your child will always prefer songs sung by a loved one! Use recordings to extend your child's musical appreciation (for example introducing them to many different instrumental sounds), and try to avoid music as background noise, as this can encourage children to switch off rather than listen.

Music Reviews

'Child's Play'
Elio

About: Child's Play is the work of Elio, an Adelaide-based composer who is skilled in creating meditative, holistic music. This music is not showy or attention seeking; rather, like a wonderful fragrance it permeates the space, filling it with a glowing, magical ambiance.

Slow-moving harmonies and a rocking pulse, help create a relaxing atmosphere - perfect for quiet play, soothing and sleeping. Many instrumental colours are used in Elio's music, introducing the young listener to a range of instruments and sounds. Woven through the peaceful harmonies are moments of playfulness and joy, which cleverly add depth to the music and inspire youthful imagination.

Age Group: Great for babies and young children.

Available at www.elio.net.au

Gift of the Tortoise
Ladysmith Black Mombazo

About: This classic children's album by the internationally renowned South African male choir group 'Ladysmith Black Mombazo' was released in 1994. It has been loved and cherished by many families worldwide.

This truly magical and transporting CD takes you on a journey: The album is a pastiche of descriptive narration, short stories and song from the group's homeland, South Africa. Gcina Mhlophe is the voice of the old tortoise, Fudugazi, who travels around South Africa unearthing stories and describing images of daily life.

Sung partly in Zulu and partly in English, the songs are representative of the Zulu style of A Capella singing. Gentle voices sing rich, sunny harmonies with dancing rhythms. A wonderful introduction to foreign songs and cultures.

Age Group: Perfect for 0-10 years (and parents!)

Handling Aggression
Part 1: The Vigorous Snuggle

Many parents struggle to know what to do when their child has an outburst ~ especially if that outburst is an aggressive one. **Rachel Schofield** *explains why children have these outbursts and provides an effective method of dealing with them*

My five year old son bent down and picked up a wooden building block. He looked up, caught my eyes, and then deliberately hurled the block at me. It whacked my leg with full force leaving me stinging in pain. Ouch!

Well meaning plans that involve deep breaths before reacting seem to fly out the window at moments like this. At best we might fruitlessly try to reason with our revved up child, "I can see you're angry but it's not okay to throw blocks, it hurts other people" or maybe we find ourselves shouting threats, "don't you dare! If you throw that block you'll have to…….," offering a consequence or time out. Events can quickly turn ugly. Things we swore we'd never do seem to happen: maybe we drag our child screaming to their room so they can learn a lesson or worse … Later we feel guilty and confused. How did things get so out of hand? Why did our darling child throw that block in the first place? And what on earth are we meant to do anyway? It can feel like something is terribly wrong with us and our child.

In truth, however loving and attentive parents are, many, if not all, children at one time or another lash out at others – whether it be hitting, biting, kicking, scratching or hurling blocks. It's tempting to think that we need to teach them that such behavior is not acceptable. But really, even very young children are quick learners. Children have excellent memories. My son certainly knew that throwing blocks with the intention of hurting me was not okay. So why did he do it?

EMOTIONS DRIVE BEHAVIOR

"Emotions drive a lot of behavior," Dr Vicky Flory, a Lecturer in Psychology reminds us, "We don't see children's emotions directly, but rather through their behavior and facial expressions". If we watch closely we can notice that aggressive outbursts, like my son's, are driven by fears that lie deep inside.

From early in life children experience many, many things that are deeply frightening to them. Major stresses such as a difficult birth and necessary medical treatments leave obvious emotional scars. But other more minor events that might seem inconsequential to the adults around also frighten a baby. A sudden loud noise, waking alone in a room, or an overly enthusiastic cuddle from an older sibling might be very scary for an infant. However attentive and attuned a caregiver is, all children get frightened. Until they are able to heal from the hurts, these fears stay lodged inside a child's emotional memory called 'implicit memory'. Dr Dan Siegel, a Professor of Psychiatry, says that "implicit memory relies on brain structures that are intact at birth and remain available to us throughout life". These memories can get re-stimulated by things that remind us of the original fright. Dan explains that if a child becomes frightened "by a loud noise associated with a particular toy they will get upset when shown that toy in the future". But they won't have a conscious memory of why they are frightened by the toy. Fears experienced early in life, even in the womb, remain with a child and are triggered again by events and situations that are reminiscent of the original fright.

So for my son there was something in that moment which ignited a deep old fear lodged in his implicit memory. He couldn't ask for help because he'd lost his sense of closeness to me. Instead the tight knot of bad feelings stuck inside made him lash out. I don't know why my son felt scared in that moment and in a way it didn't matter. I did know that it was my job to reach in and help him feel my love and help him offload the upset that was stopping him thinking.

FEAR STOPS THINKING

When we feel deeply frightened we can no longer think. We can no longer access our prefrontal cortex, the seat of reasoning and judgment in our brain. Bruce Perry, a child trauma expert, explains that when we are in a state of fear, brain scans show that there is virtually no activity in our thinking brain. So we respond with the basic mammalian response to feeling

> *'If we watch closely we can notice that **aggressive outbursts … are driven by fears that lie deep inside**'*

threatened: fight, flight or freeze. My son was going for fight. When driven by a fight response children will scratch, hit, kick as well as throw things! So my son, now feeling deep primal fear and completely unable to access his thinking brain, responded by lashing out at me.

At this point it is obvious that trying to reason with a child "hey, it's not okay to throw blocks" is futile, children cannot think in this state. Encouraging a child to use words and naming their feelings may, if we are lucky, take a child into their thinking brain and away from their primal response but does nothing to heal the fears lodged inside. The hurt will bubble up again at another moment with some other unworkable behavior. Of course shouting, punishing and doling out consequences focuses only on the behavior; these strategies pay no attention to the reasons why your child is stuck in a state of fear and they only add further hurts driving an ever deeper wedge of disconnection between parent and child. They may appear to work temporarily with younger children, but the problem behaviours come back, only next time more sneakily. So what can we do?

CONNECTING AND HEALING

It never makes sense to let a child's aggression go unanswered. We need to target the real problem: turn around the child's sense of disconnection and heal those fears stuck in our child's implicit memory. Luckily children instinctively know how to heal themselves. If we stay close to a child and offer warm loving attention they will offload the feelings of hurt that are stuck inside. They will laugh, cry, tremble or tantrum. If we can stay close as they do this we will see that as they work all the way through their messy feelings they will come out the other side much better. When they finish clearing out a big chunk of feelings they may snuggle close to us, fall into a deep sleep or even just get up brightly and carry on as if nothing happened. They will be able to think again.

In turn, as parents, we too have many emotional memories waiting to be healed. The moment our child aggressively lashes out at us, old hurts get triggered - we leave our thinking rational brain and dive deep into our emotions. The impulse we have at the moment our child lashes out tends to

be how we were treated as children. It's taped in our brains. We repeat our own parents' reactions without thinking. It doesn't matter how committed we are to being a nurturing parent: if we were lectured, we feel like lecturing; if we were hit, we feel an urge to hit. To find new ways of reacting we too have to heal our own hurts. We can do this by finding a good listener – we need someone to pay warm attention without judgment and without giving advice as we talk about our impulses and shed emotional tension. This helps clear away hurts and find new paths. Over time we will find we can use new ways of responding to our child when they lash out at us.

So back to the block moment. What happened next? Swallowing the initial fright that shot up, I moved in as warmly as I could. I said in a kind voice and with a cheeky glint in my eye, "Now that's a funny way to ask for a raspberry on the belly". I moved close towards my son trying to give him a 'vigorous snuggle'.

THE VIGOROUS SNUGGLE

Patty Wipfler, founder of the not-for-profit organization Hand in Hand Parenting, explains "You're doing what one might call a 'limbic tackle'. You can't get through to your child's prefrontal cortex, because he can't feel his connections with anyone at the moment. He can't listen to reason. So you do things his limbic system—the social center of his mind—can understand"

By making playful warm physical contact, "you stop the behaviour he's caught in, but you do it with nonverbal, generous "I want to be close to you" gestures. These are the signals that his limbic system is starved for. These are the signals that let him laugh, or let him break into a big tantrum. These are the signals that, one way or another, will get his mind working again, aware that it's safe to love and let others love him"

To begin with I found it was pretty difficult to do this. But over time it's got easier to respond with affection when my son lashes out. It helps enormously to find someone who can listen to us (out of earshot from our children) as we let loose about how cross we feel when our child hits the dog, scratches her brother, throw blocks at us etc.

So after I'd spent some time rolling around on the floor giggling with my son and trying to plant raspberries on his belly, he began to soften. The laughter had helped heal some hurts and he was feeling connected to me again. He came close and sat on my lap, put his arms round my neck, looked into my eyes and said "You're made of nice." And that was it: he played well for the rest of the afternoon.

What a turnaround! This 'vigorous snuggle' response works well for a child who hits, bites, scratches or throws things occasionally but for a child with a chronic pattern you need to embark on what Patty Wipfler describes as an 'emotional project'. The not for profit organization Hand in Hand Parenting has an online self access course 'No More Hitting!' to take you through such a project.

You might be wondering how this could work when one child lashes out at another. Really the steps are the same: move in and compassionately stop the aggression, then offer warm connection as you listen to their feelings. Except things are a bit trickier, you now have two children needing attention. In "Handling Aggression Part 2" we'll look at this in more detail, but for now you could experiment. What works best? If you're the only adult around, is it moving in and affectionately nuzzling the aggressive child first, before tending to the hurt child? Or vice versa? Or is it switching attention from one to the other and then back again?

See how it goes! I'd love to hear about your vigorous snuggle experiments and any questions you have over on the Nurture's Facebook page.

Rachel Schofield runs Building Emotional Understanding courses (online and in person) and co-moderates Hand in Hand Parenting's online discussion group. You can contact her at www.likeripples.com

To receive 10% off Hand in Hand's "No More Hitting" course, go to www.handinhandparenting.org and enter code "Nurture" at checkout

Interested in running your own business from home?

Kodomo is looking for a new owner.

Established a little over 18 months ago, Kodomo has grown from being a nappy reseller to be a supplier of a whole range of baby and children's products including organic skincare, fairtrade cotton baby clothes, rag dolls and other gifts, cloth feminine protection and of course, modern cloth nappies and accessories.

Says current owner Nyree: "I have really loved setting up Kodomo and watching it grow all while being at home with my children. I recently began a research masters degree and sadly no longer have enough time for the business."

This would be a great opportunity for anyone who has thought about running a home business to begin with established branding, newsletter list, social media presence, Google ranking and trade partners. All the hard work has been done!

Email kodomo@kodomo.com.au to find out more.

Soap Nuts

Natural - Safe - Affordable

Soap nuts are small outer shells of a berry grown on trees. Soap nuts contain saponin, a naturally foaming surfactant which acts like detergent when immersed in water. This creates a safe, natural and toxic chemical-free substitute for regular detergents.

- Lower your family's toxic chemical exposure.
- Do your laundry from as little as 10c a wash.
- Clean your home safely and effectively.
- Anti-Inflammatory, antibacterial and antimicrobial.
- Popular with cloth nappy users and those with skin irritations.

Pure Revolution

Free Shipping

www.purerevolution.com.au

SPECIAL OFFER

Purchase a copy of Dr Sarah Lantz's bestselling book and receive a FREE Miessence gift pack worth $30*

For the months of June - August 2012

miessence
the world's first certified organic skin care range

ORDER: www.chemicalfreeparenting.com
Contact: info@chemicalfreeparenting.com

The proof is in the puddin.

Each 'Lil Puddins' modern cloth nappy is a complete nappy system with no soaking, bleaching, pins or folding!

'Lil Puddins' modern cloth nappies (MCNs) are fully adjustable from newborn (3kgs) to toddler (16kgs) and come with a breathable PUL waterproof outer, 100% bamboo fibre lining, double leg gussets and a narrow crutch, for added comfort. Two 100% bamboo fibre inserts (1x long, 1x short booster) are included with every Lil Puddins MCNs. Each insert has three layers of 100% clamboo fleece, giving you up to seven layers of superior absorbency. Coupled with the natural anti-microbial and anti-fungal properties of bamboo, Lil Puddins MCNs are the only choice for your bubs bum!

Shop online at lilpuddins.com.au

Dad's Corner

One dad's adventures of natural parenting with his little buddy, William

William at his birthday party

Me and William walking hand in hand along the beach

William plum tuckered in the carrier!

Watching the sunset with my boy!

Since the last issue, our son William turned one. It is amazing that a year has gone by already. As a bloke though, I'm excited to see our boy get bigger. I can't understand why women seem to want them to stay little for longer! Now that he is bigger, I can interact with him more. He's not a blob anymore! He's, well, human!

I've been taking William, in our carrier, on walks in the bush most mornings and afternoons. We are lucky to live in an area where native wildlife abound. Rather than try to walk a set distance, I have found it better to stop and smell the roses so to speak. Sometimes when we walk, William notices spiders or wallabies so we stop and stand silently in the bush. It is amazing to see the expression on his face as each step on our walk becomes an adventure. Some mornings we walk in our garden and he touches the leaves of various plants and he seems to draw much delight from this experience too. It also provides me with a new perspective on things ~ seeing his delight and excitement makes me look at those things with fresh eyes.

We also went on a camping trip to South West Rocks in NSW. It was wonderful spending a whole week with William (and his mum!). I really notice how much we bond when I don't disappear 5 days a week for work. During our week away we went on walks along the beach, fed the ducks and watched kangaroos lazing in the sun. As we walked along the beach it was touching when William would walk up and grab my finger so we could walk together (although I have to bend down a bit which becomes a little uncomfortable after a while ~ but it's worth it!). While he had the comfort of holding mine or his mum's hand, William got used to the waves covering his feet and then washing the sand out from underneath them. It feels good that, at this stage of his life, I can provide him with the safety he needs to try these new things. And everyday he is doing new things ~ it is like watching a flower open!

I've also noticed in the last couple of months how much William wants to be of service. For example, he has watched me hitch and unhitch the caravan a couple of times and now he stands right beside me, tugging at the safety chains and trying to wind up the jockey wheel! Another example is when we flew our kite down the beach on holiday. Once it was time to drag it back in, there he was, on one end helping take it back up the beach! I never noticed things like this with my first two children. I was a lot less patient too. In these types of situations I would have told them to stand aside because I could do it much quicker on my own. Now I don't even notice the time ~ I just notice the time it allows me to spend with my little buddy. I feel blessed that I have been given a second chance to experience these things.

It's the Lonely Fruit that get Spoiled

Melanie Wright, founder of Kanga Collective, Australia's largest babywearing community, gives her take on babywearing!

"Put her down, you are SPOILING her"! Oh! How often have I heard that statement. I have three children and all have been worn physically upon my body since birth. My youngest, who is two and a half, is still worn in a carrier or a sling more often than not. Random statements from strangers really get me wondering just how we have gotten so detached from our babies. Has social conditioning really led us Westerners to this place of loneliness, where we expect that it is normal to leave our precious baby alone? Following your instincts and holding your baby is simply one of the very best gifts you can give your child. Throughout your baby wearing career you will not only create and affirm an unbreakable bond with your precious baby, you may also lessen the severity of Post Natal Depression. Breastfeeding can be established more easily and your baby will be more contented because you are close enough to attend to her needs immediately. I mean, that's the time frame that babies have – it is now or now!

Babies are born to be worn. Their bodies and minds are quite simply made for being held. Humans are known as 'Parent Clingers'. She is not a rabbit, who must stay quietly in the den while mother forages for hours (the altricial animal, who stays in the nest). Nor is she a horse, who can follow her mother almost immediately after birth (the nidifucous animal, meaning one who leaves the nest, or follows the mother, immediately after birth). Another common complaint is 'she cries as soon as I put her down'. There is a reason for this and it is innate. Babies simply need their care-giver to hold them because they feel in danger when left alone. The cry of desperation, also known as 'contact crying' is when they feel so vulnerable and unsafe that their own instinct is to cry for their caregiver. They are hard wired to be held, it is the way they are born. The way we all are born. As infants we too were Parent Clingers! Knowing all of this, how then can carrying your child be still seen as 'spoiling'? How can this be seen as anything but wonderful? I personally would like it to be seen as normal rather than wonderful! Two thirds of the world wear their babies in one way or another, the Western world being the exception. Somewhere, somehow, our way of life got in the way of our instinctual desire to hold our babies. It was Western society that deemed this the norm, that babies are manipulative because they want to be held. This is not true.

Babies bodies are made for being held. When their body rests on your hips, their bowed legs lock into your hip like a perfect jigsaw. Their legs are automatically resting in the spread-squat position, with their feet facing inward to grip furthermore. Their spine curves gently, and their head rests perfectly on your chest. Their breathing is synchronised with yours. Baby is quiet and content. The baby is actively participating in the process of being worn!

Knowing these facts make me think about our future. It allows me to ponder the possibilities for western culture should we start embracing our young! I know that wearing my babies has made them more peaceful, more accepting of what life brings and generally more contented. I also know that wearing my babies has made me happier, more confident and accepting of my new role as mother. Mother hood is not easy but the act of embracing your baby, corny as it sounds, makes it all worthwhile.

Fruit left alone gets spoiled, not babies that are held and loved. Do not ever doubt yourself or your instincts. Baby wearing puts your baby in their place – where they belong. On you.

International Baby Wearing Week is Coming in October!

The annual survey of babywearing practices in Australia by Fertile Mind is very timely, and Nurture has been given a sneak peak of some of the survey results!

At the time of printing 1500 Australian parents have responded to the survey. Over 98% of the survey participants are females; with over 40% parenting one child.

- Over 45% of the expecting mothers are planning to use a baby carrier once their baby is born
- More than half of the participants own at least one baby carrier or sling and over 40% own at least 1 pram or a stroller
- 54% of the participants are using a baby carrier at the time of answering the survey
- In 70% of the households, both parents are using the baby carrier and in more than half, they do it between hour to three a day.
- 90% of the participants feel their baby's comfort is essential when choosing a baby carrier, while only 3% list "fashionable" or the colour of the carrier as a high priority when coming to choose a baby carrier.

(The survey started on the 20th of July and will be closed on the 31st of August. The full results will be published during International Babywearing Week).

Bringing Awareness to Now

Our lives are forever getting busier and busier. Sometimes there just doesn't seem enough time to scratch our ... you know! **Emily A Filmore** *provides some guidance on how we can take control back of our moments in order to really appreciate the lives that we live.*

Breathe deeply. Live in the moment. Be present. Forget the past, don't fret about the future! Enjoy life as it unfolds.

Sounds like it should be simple doesn't it? But what does presence really mean, especially to a busy parent? It may have been easier to practice presence when you had luscious minutes (or hours) to sit in lotus chanting "OHM." But now, with the wonders and beauty of parenting, those routines may be distant memories. Do you yearn for five minutes to connect with your inner self? It's ok to admit it - there is no judgment here! Admitting it doesn't take anything away from the pleasure you experience as a parent, it is just a chance to honor the part of you that is YOU, not the YOU that is mummy/daddy; the YOU that is the wonderful, amazing, divine being who feels fulfillment when you connect with your spirituality.

But, let's be realistic, how does a busy parent find that inner calm for even a moment, much less long enough to explore the meaning of life? And if I can't, as that busy parent, find my own inner peace, how am I going to show my child how to live in the moment? I have experienced this frustration many times, have you?

In spirituality we often speak of awareness in an abstract sense: Awareness of your BE-ing-ness…Awareness of your purpose…Awareness of who you are at your soul's level. However when you become overwhelmed and busy these might feel like very BIG ideas to aspire to. So it might help to begin by focusing awareness on your surroundings, the more practical manifestations of life. Then as you move into a clearer awareness/presence with your physical surroundings, you can actually lead yourself to the more abstract type of awareness.

Many of us put a lot of pressure on ourselves to be great at everything. Even if we don't admit it, some of us even judge ourselves on our level of spirituality; we want to be great at it. We want to be great spouses/partners, we want to be great at our jobs, and, mostly, we want to be GREAT parents. Sometimes in the striving for this illusion of greatness we miss out on life's precious moments.

What do I mean by "striving for this illusion of greatness?" I mean it is an illusion that you can be anything but "great" because you are a divine being. If you are already, by nature, "divine" then there is nothing for which to strive – there is only embracing who you are. When you relieve yourself of the pressure to succeed you open yourself to just BE who you are in the moment. Your child will continue to live in the moment by your example.

It might help to take a step back and cut yourself some slack. The truth is you probably don't have time to meditate as long as you used to. You have filled your time with something equally as important and beneficial to you now, or else you probably wouldn't have chosen parenthood – your CHILD(ren). This is a natural change that accompanies the fact that you now are raising a little one. So the first step to living in the moment, is to…well…begin living in the moment by accepting that centering yourself may look different today than it did a couple of years ago. And tell yourself that this is okay! No, it is more than okay, it is a perfect manifestation of this phase of your life. (And also give yourself permission to ask for moments of alone time by asking a close friend or relative to care for your child for a few short minutes every once in a while!)

The next step is to find new ways to connect, nurture your spirit and be aware in the moment within the context of this new phase of your life. It is different at any given time, but it could mean:

- taking a walk in nature with your child;
- looking around you and SEEING colors, shapes and textures clearly;
- listening to the falling rain and truly HEARING it patter as it dances off your window pane;
- running your hand over your baby's soft, warm blanket and FEELING each bump and fluff of fuzz as it passes by your skin;
- Allowing yourself to drink in every aspect of your child's face, his smell, or the sound of her voice.

Think about the physical presence that embracing those moments will provoke within you. To take these moments from the physical to the spiritual, I think all you have to do is feel the moment fully and then express gratitude for that moment.

Another opportunity to bring your awareness to now that you may experience as a parent is in communicating with your child. Sometimes, again, because we have many things on our minds, we allow our minds to wander, going on autopilot as we care for our children. We may be bathing our child carefully, yet all the while be constructing a grocery list. We might only half listen as our three to four year old tells us a story. And a great many of us have absently responded yes to a request from a teenager, only to have our awareness dawn on what they really asked as the yes has escaped our mouths! So another practical way to bring your awareness to now might be to actively engage in the activity or conversation at hand. Not only will this ensure that you will not put a nappy on backwards or mistakenly give your child permission to go sky diving; it will also help your child to feel heard, accepted and treasured. It will illustrate for your child, by example, what it means to live in the now, to be present and how to truly listen to themselves and others.

Isn't that really all awareness means: experiencing the moment you are in without thoughts wandering to future moments, past memories, expectations or grievances? Whatever way you choose to connect with your inner BE-ingness will be perfect. Whatever amount of time you can find to devote to it will be enough. However you choose to bring your awareness to now will serve you as you desire. You can only succeed because you are the perfect manifestation of you right now!

Emily A. Filmore is the author of the With My Child series of children's books (www.withmychildseries.com) and Creative Co-Director, Conversations with God for Parents

The *With My Child* series of children's books, by Emily A. Filmore (a *Nurture* contributor), will assist you in strengthening your family bonds through simple, everyday activities!

It's a Beautiful Day for Yoga and *It's a Beautiful Day for a Walk* are must haves for your personal library.

Nurture readers receive 20% off list price when purchasing both books together at www.withmychildseries.com/nurture. Regularly Priced $35.90+p&h (USD) but *Nurture* readers get them for the discounted price of $28.72+p&h (USD)

Namaste!

Give your kids the best start in life
~ GO ORGANIC ~

As parents we all want the best for our kids - for them to be vibrant and healthy and grow and develop to their potential. Of course, one of the best ways you can do this is by feeding your kids wholesome, healthy food. But why not go one better and make it organic? Switching to organic buys you peace of mind that your family dinner and your kids' health, won't be spoiled by toxic pesticides, growth hormones, antibiotics, genetically modified ingredients or any other nasty and potentially damaging chemical additives.

5 REASONS TO BUY ORGANICS

Before you go for your next grocery shop, have a read through these 5 good reasons why you should buy organic for your family, and then make the decision whether it is worth it or not...

1. Children Are Most Vulnerable To The Effects Of Pesticide Residues In Foods

There are over 170 different types of pesticides, herbicides and fertilizers which are routinely sprayed on crops that ultimately end up in the foods we eat. Think about it. These chemicals are designed to kill insects and bugs... Research has shown that long-term ingestion of these toxic chemical residues can be harmful to our health, with children being most vulnerable. Unborn babies, infants and children are particularly susceptible to the damaging effects of pesticides due to their much smaller size and still-developing bodies. The daily consumption of small amounts of toxic residues from commercially grown foods could potentially disrupt the development and functioning of your child's immune, reproductive and nervous systems. Studies have shown that children exposed to organophosphate (OP) pesticides, especially in the womb, have a much greater chance of developing behavioural problems such as ADHD. (1) OP's are one of the most widely used pesticides in Australia and in other countries. They work by attacking the nervous system of insects, but long-term exposure in humans could cause chronic neurological problems. Organic produce is not sprayed with chemical pesticides, herbicides and fertilizers.

2. Organic Produce Contains More Nutrients And Taste

Much of the soil in Australia and other countries around the world is increasingly 'nutrient-poor' due to non-sustainable farming practices and the use of non-organic fertilizers. Perpetual farming of land can lead to soil de-nutrification. There is little doubt that through the ages of commercial farming practice, mineral depletion of soils has occurred to a significant extent and that food crops today contains fewer nutrients than in the past. Sustainable (organic) farming techniques, however, such as manuring, composting, companion planting and crop rotation ensures that the soil is healthy and has an adequate supply of nutrients from which crops can grow. Studies show that organic crops are nutritionally superior to commercially grown crops, having higher levels of all those important vitamins, minerals and antioxidants, which your kids need for healthy growth and development and protection from illness.(2) Another bonus of buying organic fruits and vegies is that your kids can eat their edible skins, which are an excellent source of dietary fibre. This is a great way to further boost their fibre intake. Organic fruits and vegies are not only better for your health because they are richer in nutrients and are chemical free, they also taste better. Organic farmers let their fruit naturally ripen before they are picked so they contain higher levels of nutrients and a richer fuller flavour. Your kids won't need to cover their fruits and vegies in sauces anymore. Help them learn to appreciate the wonderful, clean, natural flavours of fruits and vegies again.

3. Organics Are Free From Hormones And Antibiotics:

Remember that whenever you give your kids milk or other dairy products, eggs, meat, and chicken, they are also consuming the chemicals sprayed on the animals feed and the antibiotics and other

drugs given to that animal. So it is always a good idea to buy organic animal products. Most nonorganic livestock are given antibiotics and other drugs on a regular basis to maximize meat and egg production. There is growing evidence to suggest the long-term consumption of low levels of antibiotics has a detrimental effect on the development of children's immune function. Organic livestock are fed organic feed and are not given antibiotics or hormones. Organic milk is also richer in beneficial omega-3 fats, which are essential for your child's brain and nervous system development.

4. Organics Are Free From Genetic Modification

There has been insufficient research into the long-term effects of these gene altered foods on humans. It is suspected however that genetically modified foods are potentially harmful and may have a significant impact on children. Indeed, the potential health dangers in consuming GM foods are numerous. For example, GM foods might contain resistant bacteria or viruses and unlabelled allergic proteins. These may adversely affect immune function and of course, allergic sensitivity when consumed. Moreover, the extent of these changes can only be speculated upon as there is, by much estimation, insufficient understanding of the dynamic changes that take place in GM plants and little knowledge of what second and third-generation plants will produce. Certainly, the risk to children's health must surely be considerable when the possibility of immune-function type effects are considered. Crops that are commonly modified in some countries include soy beans, canola (rape seed), corn and potato. Everyday products containing GM foods include breakfast cereals, soy products and vegetable oils. Australia requires mandatory labelling of all GM foods and products containing GM ingredients. However, in some countries like America, which produces the majority of GM foods, it is not mandatory to label GM foods or products containing them. It is my sincere recommendation that, by virtue of the uncertainty surrounding GM foods and children's health, all food labels should be read carefully and products containing genetically modified foods should be avoided. The only true way to avoid genetically modified foods is to buy certified organic.

5. Better For The Environment And Helps Support Your Local Community

It's a good idea to check if you have an organic farmers market in your local neighbourhood. Not only will you be supporting your local small farmers but you will be reducing your carbon foot print and it's usually cheaper too. Also, there are lots of organic home delivery services available now which are very convenient, especially if you have young children that are difficult to stroll around the markets with.

WHAT IF YOU

www.nurtureparentingmagazine.com.au | 55

Certified organic produce.

Home delivery to Sydney Metro & Illawarra regions.

Providores of organic fruit and veggies, breads, milk, eggs, cheeses.

gift boxes & christmas hampers

www.niOrganics.com

order online

niOrganics

0432 081 454

CAN'T BUY ORGANIC ALL OF THE TIME

Ideally, we should all buy organic as much as possible. However this may not be feasible for everyone, as organic foods can be more expensive, and some may not have access to organic produce regularly. Firstly this doesn't mean you should reduce the amount of fruit and vegies you give your kids. Fruits and vegies are vital to your children's good health and they should eat a good variety of them everyday. They contain essential vitamins, minerals and antioxidants that will help your kids grow to their full potential and protect them from disease. If you can't buy organic it means that you need to be diligent with washing your fruits and vegies well.

For those times when you can't go 100% organic, you can instead prioritise your selection of organic foods to those that are most susceptible to higher levels of pesticide residues. For example:

- Thin skinned berries, tomatoes, peaches, nectarines, cherries, and grapes.
- Apples and cucumbers with wax coatings, and carrots and potatoes.
- Green leafy vegies such as spinach, kale, celery and lettuce.
- Red meat, chicken, eggs, and cow's milk.
- Soy products, that are commonly made from genetically modified soy beans.

get into ORGANICS ...

www.organicfoods.com.au

SPECIAL INTRODUCTORY OFFER!!!

we fervently believe that

Organic food is BETTER for you!!!

Organic and Quality Foods P/L is offering NEW customers a great opportunity to sample the delights of organic food at a special price !

24 YEARS of EXPERIENCE

Organic & Quality Foods P/L is Queensland's oldest Home Delivery Service SPECIALISING in ORGANIC food!

PREMIUM HOME DELIVERY SERVICE

We supply CERTIFIED Fruit/Vegetables plus a COMPLETE range of grocery, dairy & meat lines! YOUR ONE-STOP ORGANIC SUPPLIER ....

7 Refrigerated Delivery Vehicles

Organic & Quality Foods P/L (OQF) has the equipment (coldrooms, freezers & refrigerated vans) to BEST service your organic requirements!

If you spend $65 or more on your first order, OQF will

REFUND 25%

of your invoice total on 2nd delivery !!!

*** 2nd order MUST also EXCEED $65 / MAXIMUM refund of $50-00

GREAT OFFER ...
to accept simply contact OQF:
(07) 3275 3552
rob@organicfoods.com.au

TIPS FOR KEEPING CHEMICALS OUT OF YOUR KIDS DIET.

The best way to remove toxins from your child's diet is to provide organic foods whenever possible. However, when consuming commercially grown products there are ways you can reduce pesticide residue:

1. Thoroughly wash all non-organic fruit and vegetables.
2. Peel all non-organic fruit and vegetables with skins such as carrots, potatoes, pumpkin, pears and peaches.
3. Peel foods such as cucumbers and apples that have a wax coating (wax prolongs their shelf life but also seals in harmful pesticide residues).
4. Rinse non-organic rice, grains and legumes well before cooking and use fresh water to cook with. These foods are also routinely sprayed with chemicals.
5. Choose organically farmed meats, chickens and eggs where possible. If you buy non-organic meat make sure you trim all visible fat, as toxins tend to accumulate in the fat of animals. Lamb is a good choice of red meat as it generally contains less toxins than other types of meat.

REFERENCES:
(1) Chensheng Lu, Kathryn Toepel, Rene Irish, Richard A. Fenske, Dana B. Barr, and Roberto Bravo, Environ Health Perspect. Organic Diets Significantly Lower Children's Dietary Exposure to Organophosphorus Pesticides 2006 February; 114(2): 260–263. Published online 2005 September 1. doi: 10.1289/ehp.8418.
(2) Worthington V. Effect of Agricultural Methods on Nutritional Quality: A Comparison of Organic with Conventional Crops. Alternative Therapies 1998; 4: 58-69.

Lisa Guy is a homeopath and naturopath who runs 'Art of Healing' (www.artofhealing.com.au) and The Happy Baby Clinic and author of "My Goodness: all you need to know about children's health and nutrition"

Pregnancy and children's health and nutrition specialist

artofhealing
naturopathic medicine

Lisa Guy ND
Naturopath & Author

lisa@artofhealing.com.au
0414 491 595
www.artofhealing.com.au

herbal medicine • homeopathy • nutrition

Baby Led Weaning

*Most parents start their baby on purees then go to lumpy food and then eventually the child graduates to real solids. However, there is a child led approach to solids that more and more parents are choosing. It's called Baby Led Weaning ~ **Tracey Murkett** explains more*

When it comes to the way babies experience solid foods there has been a particular method that has been ingrained in our culture for generations. Everyone knows what it looks like: an adult loads up a spoonful of pureed mush and tries to persuade the baby to eat it. Sometimes the baby will try to grab the spoon, or turn away, lips closed, to avoid it. Sometimes he'll accept the food, only to spit it out soon after. And some babies will happily eat smooth purees but reject lumpy foods a few months later. Many parents feel they need to bribe, persuade or cajole their child to eat, and end up doing this throughout the toddler years.

In this scenario, it's the parents who decide when their baby tastes his first solid food, when he is ready to 'move up a stage' to lumpy foods and when he's allowed to eat family food. For most babies, the experience of solid foods is distinctly parent led.

Baby-led weaning (BLW) – also known as baby-led solids – is different. It allows babies to join in with healthy family meals from the beginning, handling real food and taking it to their mouth whenever they are ready. With this approach, babies explore food at their own pace and continue to take as much milk or formula as they want. It's up to them how much or how little they eat, and it's up to them which foods they choose from what is offered. (Weaning is used here with the British meaning: the first time a baby has anything other than milk or formula, rather than the Australian meaning of leaving the breast. The introduction of solid foods is the very first step in the gradual process of weaning from breast or bottle, which can take several years to complete.)

Baby-led weaning is based on the normal development of babies in their first year. Research shows that at around six months, babies' immune and digestive systems are ready for solids foods. At this age they are also able to sit up unaided and take objects to their mouth accurately – and they are beginning to make chewing movements. In other words, they are ready and able to feed themselves. As long as they have the opportunity, all healthy babies will spontaneously start to grab food and explore it whenever they are ready. Just like crawling, walking and talking, learning to eat solid food is a natural and inevitable part of development for any healthy baby.

This means that the spoon feeding we are all so familiar with is unnecessary. It's simply left over from the days when everyone believed that babies needed solid food at an age when (we now know) they were really too young for it. When the recommended minimum age to introduce solids changed from four months to six in 2003, few people considered how much more capable babies are by that age. The only way you can get solid foods into a baby of four months is to make it very soft and runny and spoon it in. But two months later, the same baby can feed himself. In fact, finger foods have long been recommended from around six months, so this isn't really anything new. BLW simply ditches the puree stage beforehand.

There appears to be real advantages to allowing a baby to feed himself from the beginning. Recent research from the University of Nottingham, England, shows baby-led weaning promotes long-term healthy food preferences and that babies allowed to self feed are less likely to be overweight as children than those who are spoon-fed pureed food. This apparent protection against obesity is probably due to the 'hands off' approach of BLW: babies who start solids this way are allowed to take their time with food and self regulate the amount they eat. As many parents will recognise, it's all too easy when spoon feeding to encourage babies to eat faster (which is associated with obesity in adults) and to persuade them to override their feelings of satiety by encouraging them to eat as much as you think they need. With BLW, babies eat at their own pace and simply stop eating when they feel they have had enough – however little that is. Making healthy food choices as a child is likely to come from sharing nutritious family

'baby-led weaning promotes long-term healthy food preferences and that babies allowed to self feed are less likely to be overweight as children than those who are spoon-fed pureed food'

meals from the start, and being allowed to handle and taste a variety of foods with no pressure to eat. Trusting a baby to know what he needs – even if it seems slightly eccentric to his parents – is at the heart of BLW.

There are other advantages too. Babies learn about food by experimenting and playing; the range of textures and shapes help develop manual dexterity and the ability to deal with different types of food in their mouth. Learning to chew naturally, when they are ready, helps babies to eat safely and may enhance jaw development. And most babies who start solids this way continue to have plenty of milk feeds, rather than filling up on less nutritious foods.

These advantages are compelling enough but a quick search on Internet blogs and forums reveals some simpler reasons why BLW is becoming increasingly widespread: most families find it easier, less stressful and more enjoyable than spoon feeding. The mealtime battles that seem to be so common with babies and toddlers rarely happen with BLW because no-one is fighting the baby's instinct to feed himself or trying to control what he eats. The whole family eat the same (healthy) food together so there's no need to buy or prepare separate meals, or to let your own dinner go cold while you feed the baby. Babies seem to enjoy joining in and having the chance to copy their parents or siblings.

There's no need for a baby's experiences of food to be parent led. Baby-led weaning is natural and common sense - you can simply trust your baby's instincts to feed himself and follow his lead.

THE BASICS OF DOING BABY-LED WEANING:

How to start:

- Prepare for mess! Food will be dropped, squished and squeezed as your baby learns how to handle it. A clean splash mat under the chair means you can re-offer dropped food.
- As soon as your baby can sit up with little or no support, sit her on your lap or in a highchair at family mealtimes. Make sure she can reach the food easily.
- Choose times when your baby isn't tired or hungry – mealtimes are for learning and exploring to start with. Remember the motto 'food before one is fun'.
- Let her share the food on your plate, or put a few pieces of food in front of her for her to pick up (a plate of her own may be distracting).
- Offer your baby water to drink with her meals – but don't be surprised if she isn't interested. If she's breastfed, she may prefer to continue to have all her drinks at the breast.
- Continue to offer breastfeeds or formula on demand.

Foods to offer:

- Thick sticks of food will be easiest for your baby to hold at first – long enough for a bit to poke out from her fist. Most healthy family food is suitable, such as fruit, vegetables, cheese or large strips of meat (for sucking or chewing). Aim for variety – your baby will enjoy learning how to handle different textures. She'll move on to using spoons and forks gradually.
- Offer a variety of flavours – babies don't need bland food. Unless there are allergies in your family there is

no need to start with one taste at a time.

• Avoid salt, ready-meals, junk food and additives as much as possible (you may need to check labels carefully – some common foods, such as baked beans and gravy can be very high in salt). Honey and undercooked eggs carry a small risk of food poisoning so they should be avoided until your baby is over a year old.

What to expect:

- At first your baby will grab pieces of food and explore them with her hands. Then she'll taste it. Before long she'll start to bite and chew it and a week or two later she'll start swallowing it.
- Mealtimes are for playing and learning, at first, so your baby probably won't eat much for the first few months. Provided she can breastfeed or have formula whenever she wants, her milk feeds will continue to provide all her nourishment.
- Many babies gag on food in the early weeks. (see insert box for discussion on gagging).

Remember to:

- Keep mealtimes enjoyable – let your baby play and don't hurry her or try to persuade her to eat more than she wants.
- Trust your baby to cut down her milk feeds whenever she is ready.
- Explain how baby-led weaning works to anyone involved in feeding your baby.

Keep it safe:

- Make sure your baby is sitting upright to eat, not leaning back or slumping, so that she can control the food in her mouth safely.
- Don't put anything in your baby's mouth for her – and don't let anyone else do so either (watch out for 'helpful' toddlers).
- Don't offer your baby hard nuts; remove stones from food such as olives and cherries; cut small round fruits, such as grapes, in half.
- Never leave your baby alone with food.

Tracey Murkett is co-author of 'Baby-led Weaning, Helping your baby to love good food', 'The Baby-led Weaning Cookbook,' and 'Baby-led Breastfeeding, How to make breastfeeding work with your baby's help' published by Vermilion.

www.buyhealthy.com.au

Keep your house free of dangerous chemicals – buy eco-friendly natural products!

Household Cleaning
Dishwashing
Laundry
Personal Care
Pet Care

from leading brands:
Back to Basics, Citrolife, ecostore, enviroCare, enviroClean, Herbon

Eat healthy, natural and organic food!

Coconut and flaxseed oils, Dry Fruits, Kapai Puku, Natural and Gluten Free Cereal and Muesli

from leading brands:
Flip Shelton, lovingearth, Niulife, Tabletop Grapes, Waihi Bush, WBC

Save money by buying in BULK!

Save time with home delivery!

Save environment by reducing packaging rubbish!

Expect some gagging – but not choking!

Many babies gag on food in the early weeks. This is a normal protective reflex and it's not the same as choking – although they are sometimes confused. Gagging is a retching movement that pushes food forward if it goes too far back in the mouth before it's ready to be swallowed. The gag reflex is more sensitive in babies than in adults and is triggered further forward on the tongue – well before it gets to the point where an adult would gag and long before the baby's airway is threatened. It's likely that the gag reflex is a safety mechanism that teaches babies to eat safely. It doesn't seem to bother them, and once the food has been pushed forward, either it falls out of their mouth or they carry on chewing it.

Gagging

Very occasionally, a piece of food may 'catch' in the baby's throat and she'll cough and splutter. She may go red in the face and her eyes may water. This is often referred to as choking but it is not life-threatening and the baby will usually clear the problem herself within a few seconds. Patting her on the back won't help and may even make things more difficult for her – your role is to be calm and reassuring while she sorts it out.

Choking

True choking is very rare. It occurs when the airway is completely blocked and no air can get past. There is no retching movement or coughing and the baby will need urgent help to clear the obstruction. However, provided basic safety rules are followed (see box), babies are no more likely to choke if they feed themselves than they are if they are spoon fed. All parents – whatever method of introducing solids they choose – should attend a first aid course to learn how to identify and deal with a true choking episode.

WHAT'S COOKING?

Recipes to cook for the kids and with the kids!

Baby-Led Weaning Recipe

Spicy Lamb Patties with Couscous

Ingredients:

500g lean minced lamb
8 cloves (or 1 tsp ground cloves)
12 cardamom pods (or 2 tsp ground cardamom)
4/5cm piece of fresh ginger, peeled and grated to finely chopped
1/2 tsp turmeric
1/2 tsp ground cumin
approx 1/2 tsp chilli powder (to taste)
30-50g breadcrumbs (1 slice of bread)
1 egg, beaten
2 tbsp thick (Greek) natural yogurt
1 packet of instant couscous
oil for frying (optional)

Preparation:

Lamb Patties

1. Use a knife to split open the cardamom pods and put the seeds into a mortar with the cloves (discard pods). Grind to a powder.
2. Transfer the powder to a large bowl and add all the remaining ingredients except the egg, yogurt and oil. Mix well.
3. Add the egg and yogurt and miz thoroughly, so that everything is bound together.
4. Shape the mixture into small patties (flouring or wetting your hands will help to stop it sticking), making sure they are all roughly the same thickness.
5. If you have time, cover them and put them in the fridge to firm up for an hour or so.
6. Heat a frying pan, and add a little oil (if needed).
7. Fry the patties for 5-10 minutes on each side, until cooked through and browned.
8. Serve warm, with salad, couscous and roasted vegetables or rice.

Couscous

Couscous is very quick and easy and makes a nice change from rice or pasta. Most couscous sold in supermarkets is the 'instant' type, which cooks very quickly, just by adding boiling water. (Plain couscous is better than the flavoured varieties, as these often have salt added to them).

Couscous Options:
Try mixing some finely chopped onion or garlic into the dry couscous before adding the water, or stir in some chopped fresh herbs just before serving.

Cooking with Kids Recipe

Sugar Free Banana Cake

Ingredients:

Butter or oil for greasing
100g self-raising wholemeal flour
1/2 tsp ground mixed spice
50g butter (preferably unsalted)
75g raisins (or chopped figs)
200g mashed banana (1 1/2 - 2 medium sized ripe bananas)
50g walnuts, ground or finely chopped (optional)
1 egg, beaten

Topping
200g cream cheese
50-100g 100% fruit spread or jam (optional)

Preparation:

1. Preheat oven to 180oC.
2. Lightly grease a 450g loaf tim
3. Sift the flour into a large bowl and add the spices
4. Cut or break the butter into small cubes and add it to the flour.
5. Using your hands, rub the butter into the flour until the mixture looks like fine breadcrumbs
6. Stir in the raisins (or figs) and make a well in the centre of the mixture.
7. In a separate bowl, mash the banana, add the walnuts (if using) and stir in the egg.
8. Pour the banana mixture into the flour mixture and fold in
9. Put the mixture into the loaf time and put in the oven.
10. Turn oven down to 160oC and bake for 45-60 minutes, or until done)
11. Remove the tin from the oven and allow to cool for 5-10 minutes, then turn out onto a wire rack to cool
12. Serve plain, with creme fraiche or nature yogurt of covered with the topping.
13. To make the topping, combine ingredients and mix thoroughly, then spread evenly over the cake.

Recipes extracted from *'The Baby-Led Weaning Cookbook'* by Gill Rapley & Tracey Murkett, published by Vermilion

Finding Peace Inside & Out

Finding peace in this fast paced world can be difficult. However, because life is so fast paced, it is all the more important to find peace. **Sarah Cody** *explains the benefit of meditation and how you can help your children find peace through meditation.*

The world is a busy place these days and whether a child is mostly home with a parent, or in school, it is likely that they are constantly on-the-go, from one activity or errand to another, quickly processing experiences and information. While modern thought often suggests therapy and medication that may work, there is actually an ancient solution that is more of a certainty as well as longer-lasting – Meditation.

Surprisingly, children often have an easier time with meditation than adults. They don't carry the same mental baggage that adults do. And they are more open to understanding and believing the abstract – that human beings are more than just the physical body and mind. Call it spirit, qi, energy or something else, but there is something that holds the true essence of who we are, and also connects us to other people and the natural world around us. We know when our body is injured because it sends a message to our brain and we feel the sensation of pain. But we have lost touch with our ability to sense an imbalance in our 'Subtle System' (see picture) – or have we? When you have had a hectic week and nothing seems to be going right, do you feel upset in your gut area? This is a physical manifestation that tell us our subtle self is out of balance. The Subtle System is connected to our physical body. We get those messages when we've really let things go out of balance. Meditation is a way to set aside everything that stands in the way of letting us be more sensitive to the needs of our subtle self – all thoughts, wants, problems – if even for brief periods of time. And we come out feeling less bothered by petty issues and overall, refreshed. It's the same for our kids. Children who practice meditation report less anxiety (for example, regarding tests at school), a better ability to manage intense emotions like sadness and anger, and more positive relationships.

While meditation can be done anywhere, it helps to have a special place in the home where you and your child can feel peaceful and where there are less distractions for busy hands and minds. Have your child help you create a special area for meditation. It can be as simple as clearing a bedside table and adding a pretty cloth and some natural elements – flowers, shells, leaves. Put a small rug or blanket down to create a space to sit. Creating a defined area with boundaries can help keep the mind from wandering and keep it just how we want it – at peace. This space also becomes a place a child can come to when he or she needs some tranquility.

If you want to practice meditation as a family, then have everyone talk about what time of day you can all set things aside and come together to meditate. As with anything, making it a routine ensures that you will do it. You brush your teeth morning and night to keep them clean and healthy, don't you? Well, meditation is just as good for you, if not more! Maybe your daily routine allows you to sit together in the morning before the buzz of day begins, or in the evening as everyone tries to settle down before bedtime. You will guide your child to meditation. It can be difficult for you to be in meditation at the same time. But once you have finished with the guided piece, adults can do their own meditation and your children will benefit from seeing you meditate as well. When children see you enjoying an activity, they are more likely to imitate and participate. You can invite them to sit with you, or put together a basket of quiet activities for them to do, such as mandalas to color or some beading while you are meditating.

It is also important to remember that meditation should not be a punishment or consequence. And it takes time. It can absolutely soothe unrest and a troubled mind but you will work up to that. A child that has an innate understanding of the ways that meditation makes him feel better will, eventually, even practice it on his own.

Infants and toddlers live constantly

'in the moment' so meditating with them can be as simple as having them sit with you – out in Nature works well – and in a calm, quiet voice, pointing out some of the subtle sounds you hear, the wind, some birds. Don't analyze or talk too much, just bring their attention to elements of Nature that they might overlook when busy moving and chatting.

For older children, you can give them more structure. Sitting still is a common challenge when meditating with children. Be sensitive to how your child is feeling before asking them to join you for meditation. If they are very hungry, sleepy or agitated, it will be hard for them to go past these needs and enjoy moments of silence. Especially when your children are very young and when just starting, find a time when their physical and mental needs have been taken care of. Keep in mind that it is okay to keep meditation time brief in the beginning. Even two minutes can be a good start. It should be enjoyable, not forced. Still, having said that, sometimes the adult needs to create some rules at first, as guidance. Let your child know that you will keep track of time.

A simple meditation can look like this:

- Invite your child to join you in the meditation space and sit comfortably; crossed-legged is a good position, so that the base of the spine touches the ground.
- Take a few deep breaths to bring the attention inside. After a few controlled breaths, you can just put your attention on your breath, breathing – an action we do naturally – without thinking about it.
- Put your attention at the base of your spine, where you are rooted to the ground. Slowly let your attention travel up your spine until it reaches the top of your head.

- Close your eyes.
- Settle your attention to be in the present moment. If a thought about what you did this morning or what you need to do tomorrow comes to you, let it pass. Don't follow it or get upset that it interrupted you. Keep your attention at the top of your head.
- Enjoy the silence you discover.
- After 2, 5, 10, or 15 minutes open your eyes. Keep your vision soft and your body still for another few moments and try to hold onto that silence within even as you get up and move on with your day.

Let the meditation last as long as you and your child are comfortable. Don't give up if either of you can't let go of your thoughts easily. Cultivating a quiet mind takes mental effort and as with any exercise, practice helps! Each time you sit to meditate, try to hold onto the silence for a little bit longer. Soon you will find that you are both more comfortable with it.

Once you create a connection with that inner silence, you know where to find it again. Whenever you find your child getting flustered or frustrated, remind her to take a moment to pause whatever she is doing, bring her attention to the top of her head, and then carry on. Our mind is very useful but it can get too caught up in planning and accomplishing things, and 'me, me, me!' that we forget to exist in the moment. As parents, we want to nourish our children in every way possible – body, mind, and spirit as well.

Sarah Cody has completed a Masters of Education focusing on Birth to Three, Development and Intervention. She is also a Child Development Specialist and Certified Baby Planner.

Modern Cloth Nappies... We've got you covered

Offering you a beautiful range of Modern Cloth Nappy options along with great eco friendly baby products.

Whether you are passionate about the environment or just after a gorgeous yet sustainable product for bub, we have a lovely range of eco/organic goodies for you to choose from.

We proudly stock the following brand plus more!

GroVia, itti bitti, Nifty Naps, Designer Bums, Tots Bots, bubblebubs, Little Bean Organics, GroVia, itti bitti, Nifty Naps, Jack n Jill Organic Teeth Hygiene, Designer Bums, Tots Bots, bubblebubs, Little Bean Organics.

Special offer for Nurture Magazine Readers

Munchkin Bunz would like to offer all Nurture Parenting Magazine readers a 10% discount. For our first 10 orders using the code we will pop in a bonus itti bitti Ultimate Wipe. Code NPM10

www.munchkinbunz.com.au | www.facebook.com/munchkinbunz | info@munchkinbunz.com.au

Avoiding Mastitis

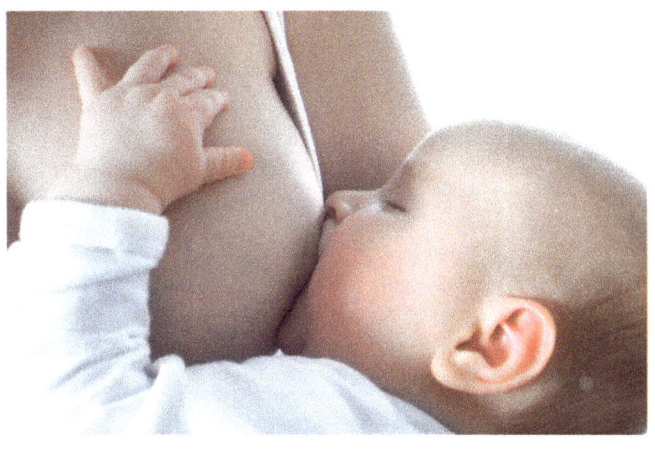

Kate Hale, RN, CM, IBCLC, discusses the two types of mastitis and how to treat them

Mastitis is one of those nasty side affects of breastfeeding, with a better understanding of it though, you can help to either fully avoid it or get over it much more quickly.

There are two types of mastitis: Bacterial Mastitis and Blocked Duct Mastitis.

BACTERIAL MASTITIS

This mainly occurs in the early stage of your breastfeeding. It is caused by a bacterial infection from bugs that get into grazes and cracks on the nipple.

Symptoms are aches, pain, flu like symptoms, temperature and a sore, inflamed breast with blotchy pink areas.

Treatment

1. As this form of mastitis is bacterial, you need to see your doctor as soon as possible and begin antibiotics (it is safe to continue breastfeeding whilst taking the antibiotic).
2. You may also need to see a lactation consultant to ensure your 'attachment' is correct, as that is usually the cause of grazes and cracks

BLOCKED DUCT MASTITIS

This can occur at any time. It is caused by a kink in a milk duct, often because of too tight a bra, wearing a bra overnight, your own elbow in the side of your breast as you sleep, by being very full from missing a feed, or sometimes it will happen when your baby sleeps for a long stretch overnight! When the milk is unable to flow towards the nipple there becomes a backlog up the ductal system that needs to drain. When it doesn't drain, the milk oozes into the tissue layer causing the pinkness, temperature etc.

The more you ' learn' your breasts by feeling them for areas of milk fullness and emptiness, the more you will be able to quickly notice an unusually firm, lumpy area and the sooner you can try to massage out the lump. By doing that you will mostly avoid a blocked duct mastitis.

The symptoms of blocked duct mastitis are similar to bacterial mastitis. You may have aches, pains, flu like symptoms, temperature and a sore inflamed breast. The breast is the difference though, there will be a large area of pinkness and in that area will be a firm lump.

Treatment

1. In the first 24 hours, try to unblock the blockage. Try to:
   - Put a warm pack on your breast for five minutes or have a warm shower.
   - When placing your baby on the breast, try and angle your baby's chin towards the lump as best as possible.
   - During every feed, massage the area of firmness from beyond it, massaging towards your nipple until your breast is soft.
   - Feed your baby often on the blocked side. Do not ignore the other side though, you might need to use a breast pump on that side if your baby is not needing both sides for each feed.
2. If the blockage is still there after 24 hours, you will need to see your doctor for antibiotics. That is because there is a chance that the blocked milk is growing bacteria. However, the antibiotics will not unblock the blockage, you still need to work on it and massage the lump as the baby feeds from that side.

happy mums happy bubs

NEW 1 hour 20 min Breastfeeding & Baby Care DVD with Midwife & Lactation Consultant, Kate Hale

DVD includes in-depth information on:

Attachment, breastfeeding, breastmilk, mastitis, baby massage & bath, dressing & wrapping your baby and much, much more.

www.happymumshappybubs.com.au

Nurturing Freedom

*"You have your way. I have my way.
As for the right way, the correct way, and the only way…
It does not exist"*

Friedrich Nietzsche

Whether it is the simple freedom of choosing what we will wear today or a complex freedom concerning our human rights – it is the privilege of making our own choices and the ability to carry them out that will leads us to being true to ourselves and loving ourselves and our own uniqueness.

Freedom to be ourselves is precious. Being loved just as we are is a stepping-stone to freedom.

To truly experience freedom we have to be free to choose. We have many choices to ponder as a parent regarding the spiritual, emotional, social and physical health of our child and family. As a parent our freedom is to choose the parenting style that aligns with who we are and what we value. These choices can be varied and difficult. However, they are also such beautiful freedoms we can embrace and treasure.

For our children freedom can seem simple. It can mean to choose their friends, clothing, food and entertainment, to ask questions, to take risks, to experiment, to push the boundaries in order to discover who they are (even if we don't always like it!).

Appreciate your freedom and help your child on their journey to discovering the choices that are theirs to make.

YOUR CHOICE. YOU DECIDE

There is freedom in choice. Giving your child options will build their choice making muscles. Choices give us a sense of personal power and autonomy. Choices help us learn to trust ourselves. But it takes practice. Children can only get practice by being given choices and the opportunity to make decisions.

Start as early as possible. Hold out two spoons and encourage your baby to choose one. Ask your child if they want to wear long pants or short pants today? Do they want to sleep with their teddy or their dragon? Do you want to play a game or listen to some music? Would you like an apple or some grapes?

It is well known that too many choices can confuse children. However, manageable and simple choices can expand your child's experiences and you can vary the range of choices as they develop.

With enough guidance and practice your child will have more confidence to make "effective" choices as a teenager – particularly when those choices don't necessarily align with their peers.

I SAY YES!

During some stages of your child's life you may feel like you are forever "redirecting" their behaviour.

One way to feel free as a parent is to have fun saying 'YES'. Forget 'societal rules' for a while and just be free to have fun – together.

Create a memory album with all your 'I SAY YES' moments (our album is full of nudey runs in the rain, wearing dress-ups out for dinner, eating cake for breakfast, staying up way past bedtime, star gazing in the middle of winter, jumping in the pool with your clothes on, playing a trick on Aunty Linda). Following your child's lead and going with the flow can be all it takes. These occasions help us lighten up, have fun and to feel safe to rebel against our norm. When you think back to your own childhood, it is these occasions that we often remember.

YAY FOR THE GREAT OUTDOORS

Getting outside is such a freeing experience – even if the air is a bit crisp. We feel rejuvenated, rested and energised by a play in the park, at the beach or a run in the back yard. Seeing the beauty of nature: grass, trees, flowers and animals, can help our children to feel free within their whole body and world.

Pottering in nature is freedom personified. Allow your child the time to play, explore and discover.

FREE TO BE YOU

As Dr Seuss so beautifully reminds us in his book 'Happy Birthday to me':

"No one has ever been born who is just like you! There is no one alive who is youer than you!"

Your smile, your touch, your tenderness and your warmth, are all unique to you. Enjoy and love being who you are and all that it brings to you and your family. Embrace the freedom you have to choose the kind of parent you want to be! Watch in awe as your child expresses their freedom to make choices and be the amazing and unique person they are destined to be.

Mumpreneur Interview
~ Successful mums tell of starting and running their own business ~

This issue we spoke to Melinda Bito, owner of Eco Toys:

What did you do prior to starting your business?
I worked for World Vision and community services related jobs such as child protection and disability services.

What inspired you to start your work-at-home business?
The birth of my daughter Safari. I wanted to be a full time mum and enjoy every precious moment so the idea of starting up a home based business really appealed to me.

Did you find it difficult starting out?
Not really, I knew exactly what I wanted to do and had the determination to make it succeed.

How many children do you have at home and what are their ages?
I've just given birth to a beautiful boy and my daughter is now 5 ½ years.

How do you juggle family and your business?
With lots of support from my husband who is also my partner in the business and from family and friends. I work whenever I can (early starts and late nights!) but also take every opportunity I can to just 'be' with my family.

What are your biggest challenges?
Definitely finding the balance to get all my work done as well as look after my family.

What advice do you have for mums wanting to start their own work-from-home business?
Have a plan, set a goal and go for it! Be realistic and most importantly be professional at all times.

Harmony Cards for Kids
...and the people in their lives

* Acceptance * Cleanliness * Compassion * Confidence * Cooperation * Creativity * Encouragement * Enthusiasm * Excellence * Fairness * Flexibility * Forgiveness * Freedom * Friendliness * Generosity * Gentleness * Gratitude * Happiness * Independence * Kindness * Love * Optimism * Patience * Peacefulness * Persistence * Purpose * Respect * Tact * Togetherness * Trust

30 illustrated cards and accompanying booklet for exploring virtues and inspiring values

Raising kind, happy and resilient kids!

Harmony Cards for Kids are a wonderful tool to help us acknowledge and share the things we admire and like about each other.

A practical and fun way to help children make meaningful connections and recognise their strengths and virtues in day-to-day life.

Order online here:
www.kidsinharmony.com.au

A Truly Nurturing Education ~ Part 2

This is Part 2 of a 4 part series on how to truly nurture your child's education. In this Part, Dr Andrew Seaton discusses the need for relevance, purpose and fun in learning. He also provides everyday activities that you can use to nurture your child's learning of language.

There are some valuable sensitivities, qualities and abilities that we can nurture in our children, which schooling is hard-pressed to support. In part one (issue 1) of this four-part article, I described one example of how parents and grandparents can nurture the fuller functioning of children. We can encourage and guide children in acting on the world around them. We can give them lots of rich and authentic experiences, engaging in self-selected activities in real-world contexts. When we do, our children are better able to think, learn and do for themselves. Just as importantly, they are also better able to retain into adulthood their intense wakefulness, enthusiasm and creativity. They are much better prepared to live intimately and dynamically connected with the world.

THE NEED FOR RELEVANCE

Many valuable skills can be developed in the context of such real world projects, including literacy and numeracy skills. Young people learn for themselves at an early age the complex structure of spoken language. Have you ever wondered, then, why so many children still struggle with written language after ten or more years of schooling? The answer has to do with the relevance to their own lives that young people see, or don't see, in literacy.

Children become proficient language users through a rich exposure to interesting and purposeful language use. They master it, when they want to. Just as with oral language learning, we do not need to obsess over explicitly teaching children the core structure of written language. Nor do we need to be preoccupied with trying to improve a child's language use. This only tends to produce feelings of inferiority in the child, to create a self-concept of 'incompetent language user', and to inhibit their use of language.

THE VALUE OF PURPOSE, FEELING AND FUN

Unless there is some specific disability, children will readily internalise language in the context of interesting and purposeful activities, and an emotionally rewarding atmosphere. Other forms of literacy, such as numeracy, visual literacy and computer literacy, are acquired and developed in similar ways. For young children, the purposefulness may simply be the fun they have in the interaction. A child's consciousness is more strongly characterised and influenced by feelings than by rational and analytical processes. The various forms of literacy are, fundamentally, communication. They are developed most effectively, not in formal contexts of mass instruction, but in interactions experienced in authentic contexts and as parent/mentor and child resonate with each other. Such relationship quality is crucial to a truly nurturing education.

When working with print-based text, children need to know the symbol system of language. They need to become able to 'decode' text, and to use the symbol system to make or 'encode' texts. They must be familiar with the letters of the alphabet, and aware of letter-sound relationships (phonics) and how letters/sounds combine to form words. Such awareness contributes to the ability to recognise words, to build vocabulary and to spell. An awareness of the conventions of sentence and paragraph structure and text layout also strengthens the child's ability to decode and encode written text. However, it is important that parents do not allow analysis of language codes to dominate the child's orientation to language. Don't let it inhibit their spontaneous and intuitive acquisition, understanding and use of language.

For example, when your young child expresses themselves orally about an observation, need or personal interest or experience, you can occasionally write the words your child has spoken. You can then read them aloud, followed by the child. You can then encourage your child to write the words as phrases, sentences and paragraphs. In this way, your child will begin to see written language as a useful extension of their own power of speech. However, it is important not to make the activity serious, or to over-verbalise or over-analyse language and

> *'Children become proficient language users through a rich exposure to interesting and purposeful language use. They master it when they want to'*

other symbol systems.

Language learning can also be facilitated if you regularly read to your child from a young age. Book selection is important. Choose stories and non-fiction books that the child finds fun or engaging. When selecting books that are related to the child's interests and talents, and ones that are uplifting and inspiring, that stir the young soul.

Another useful activity is to 'think aloud' occasionally. This can identify elements of the language code and also model specific strategies for making meaning from the book. For example, you might stop and 'think aloud' about an unusual letter-sound relationship you come across in a text. "Ah, I see! The 'fff' sound that is usually made by the letter 'f', like in the word 'funny', can also be made by the letters 'ph', like in this word 'phone'." You might occasionally 'sound out', syllable by syllable, a word that is long or unfamiliar (even if only unfamiliar to the child). You might 'think aloud' about the context of an unfamiliar word to clarify its meaning. Or you might occasionally re-read a sentence, to gain further clarity on its meaning.

Children can also be given lots of opportunities to have fun with sounds and words in games, and in hearing and creating rhymes, limericks and riddles. Here's one example of a game that connects decoding with making meaning. Take a sentence spoken by your child, and write it in large letters on some thin cardboard. Say, for example, "The rider fell off when the horse jumped over the log". Then cut each word out. Arrange the order of the words to show the original sentence. Read it aloud and ask your child, "Does this make sense?" Then re-arrange the words. For example, "the-log-fell-the-off-jumped-the-over-when-rider-horse". Read it out loud, pointing to the words as you go, then

DEEP INTELLIGENCE

Many parents, teachers and education academics are strongly sensing the inadequacies of schooling and the deeper possibilities of human functioning, but are frustrated by the lack of a coherent and comprehensive rationale or framework to rally around.

'Deep Intelligence' provides one.

It presents strong and coherent evidence concerning the ways in which human beings can function more fully than we typically do, and it outlines the kinds of activities, experiences and relationships needed to awaken and nurture them.

This book will stir and delight, challenge and inspire!

~~$39.95~~ **$27.95 SAVE 30% OFF RRP**

To order visit:
www.andrewseaton.com.au

ask your child if it makes sense? Why not? (Don't look for a technical reason!) Make several other re-arrangements, with possibly some others that do make sense. For example, "the-horse-fell-over-when-the-rider-jumped-off-the-log". "Does this make sense?" "Yes!" Lots of laughter and useful language learning will result from this language game.

DEVELOPING SKILLS THROUGH USE IN AUTHENTIC CONTEXTS

Many of these activities with various forms of literacy can be contextualised within a child's real world projects. As the child undertakes their projects, they will find the need to engage with a wide variety of texts or procedures. We can think of these as 'genres'. A genre, as I use the term here, is any purposeful activity, spoken, written or acted out, which is typically done in a particular way, or in a particular sequence. For example, conducting an experiment, sending an email, making a telephone inquiry, buying something in a shop, and even playing a game of tennis, are each distinctive genres. An understanding of genres helps us to recognise and use language and procedures appropriate to particular situations. It helps us to participate effectively in the social and material world.

As your child finds the need to engage with a particular genre, you can model its construction and 'deconstruction', to ensure that the child becomes familiar with ways in which that genre may be used. When appropriate, you might draw comparisons with experiences the child may have had previously with similar genres. It can be very helpful (to both child and parent) to have some genre guides which include a statement of the purpose of the genre, a simple outline of its typical structure, a brief description of its characteristic language features and conventions, and a short example.

EXPLAINING TEXTS AND PROCEDURES

To illustrate what I mean, let's look at a letter of thanks. The purpose of a letter of thanks could be described as follows. An expression of appreciation may take a spoken form (a 'vote of thanks') or written form (in a letter or email). Its purpose is to express thanks to one or more people, or to an organisation, for some valued contribution, assistance or consideration. The description I will give here is of a written letter of thanks such as might be sent to a person not well known personally, rather than to a familiar friend or relative.

The basic structure of a letter of thanks consists of four parts:

1. Initial details, including sender's address, date, recipient's name and address, and greeting.
2. The actual comments of appreciation are expressed, including a statement regarding the nature, time and place of the event or situation which formed the context for the help provided. Some indication might be given of how you or others benefited from the help provided. Also, recognition should be given of the efforts, time, expense or inconvenience experienced by the person, as appropriate.
3. A brief statement of well-wishing, or possibly of further association or involvement with them in the future, is generally made in conclusion.
4. Formal sign-off, including identification of the group or organisation you represent, if appropriate.

What particular language features and conventions characterise a letter of thanks? Well, it takes a polite, semi-formal tone. It is written in a mixture of present and past tenses. It makes use of full sentences and paragraphs. Paragraphs in typed letters are typically separated by a blank line. In handwritten letters the start of the first line of each new paragraph is usually indented. Linking words and phrases to do with description, benefits and thanks are used, such as "it was good to", "we learned a lot", "we appreciated", "thanks again".

(There are fifteen genre guides in my book, 'Deep Intelligence: Giving our Young the Education they Really Need'.) According to your child's need and readiness, provide a genre guide and spend some time discussing and modelling the genre and the processes and thinking that go into its construction. On occasion, you might even work with your child to create a genre guide.

The literacies and procedures outlined above really constitute the generic elements of a dynamic life. They have nothing to do with the mastery of abstract bodies of school knowledge. The end and means of such activities is not learning, as such, but the cultivation of purposeful and effective doing and interaction in the social and material world. Such activities enhance children's ability to function intuitively, to think practically and to act creatively in relation to their deeply felt interests and purposes.

I have explained above that mastery of various literacies, skills and procedures requires that a child sees relevance in those things for their own lives. However, what is really needed is much more than the perception of a merely practical relevance. A child must also sense a relevance to something in their inner core, to their deeper wisdom and guidance. This is why self-selection of real world projects is preferable and, in any case, genuine ownership and engagement are essential.

In part three of this article, we will consider some other kinds of activities, experiences and relationships which can help a child to shake off conditioning and learn to experience a deep sense of self-as-connected-with-all-life. We will look at how a truly nurturing education can help a child to feel and trust their intuition, to see things freshly, and to focus their creative energy with intention.

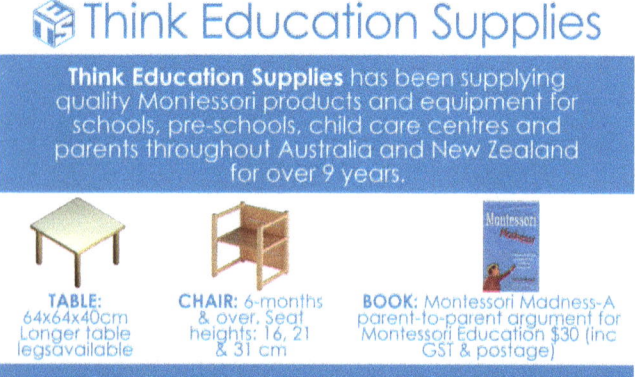

After teaching in primary and secondary schools, Dr Andrew Seaton worked in school-based and district-based advisory and leadership capacities. He has been a university lecturer in education, and has done extensive consultancy work in educational change. Andrew's Ph.D. thesis titled, 'Investing in Intelligence: An Inquiry into Educational Paradigm Change', was completed at Deakin University in 2005. His website is at www.andrewseaton.com.au

CREATIVE STORY WRITING

A great way to have fun with your child and get to know him or her on a deeper level is to share activities in which they have a chance to use their creativity! Try creating a story together.

Supplies:
You need:
- Paper, markers or crayons, a pencil
- Both of your imaginations!
- (You can also use a computer to type the story, but while it makes the recording of the story more efficient, it might detract from the fun of the process)

Leave Behind:
- Our need for perfection, our need for control, any expectation of any outcome – just enjoy the process!

Make it:

1. Ask your child what story he has in his head that he has been waiting to tell. Of course, the answer will vary greatly from child to child and if you ask the same child the same question 10 times in a day you are likely to get 10 different answers!
2. If the child is older, invite her to write the story in her own hand while you participate and listen. For younger children, ask them to recite the story to you verbally while you commit it to paper. Either way, ask your child to include you in the creative process.
3. When my daughter and I do this activity we write a few sentences on each piece of paper, we draw pictures below the words that illustrate the story and then at the end we staple the pages together to form a book - complete with a title page with her name as the author/illustrator. She gains a wonderful sense of accomplishment in having a finished product.
4. If your child gets stuck on a part of the story ask questions to help him flesh that part out. I try to do as little directing of the story as possible, allowing her to truly have ownership of the end result. If things don't make sense to you, it is okay! Remember the point is not the end result of a complete story which makes sense; the point is more about the time together and learning from, and about, each other.

Our last story had a combination of princesses, knights, monsters and rainbows. While as we wrote the story I felt it was scarier than I would choose, I let go of my need to control it and let it unfold as she chose. In the end I was pleasantly surprised to see all the strife she put into it was resolved with love, kindness and peace. So in the end I learned about the way she processes her fears, how she overcomes conflict within, how she maintains her own inner feeling of safety, and in effect, I learned more about how much love she has to share with the world.

This is a great bonding activity for many reasons: not only will your child feel treasured from the time spent together, you will also learn about the world existing inside the mind and heart of your child, you will also teach your child to embrace his or her creativity, to think outside the box, and to follow a thought through to a conclusion including a finished product; all while having fun together and creating a beautiful memory!

I hope you enjoy this story writing activity; I would love to hear from you about your shared experiences and the stories you create together. info@withmychildseries.com

Emily Filmore has written a number of books focusing on bonding with your child. You can save 20% off these books if you purchase from www.withmychild.com/nurture

Organic Gardening

Sowing the Seeds of Love
Propagation for little people

WHERE DO ONIONS COME FROM?

You'd be surprised how many children and even adults are not quite sure the answer to this question. Understanding how plants grow, where they come from, and how to propagate your own is not only a very handy cost effective way to have more plants but it is also super important to the developing mind of a child to have an understanding of where and how things green come to be.

Spring is one of the best and most rewarding times to give propagating plants a go. Whether it is from seeds, bulbs or cuttings, even the newest and littlest to gardening can have success with the right choice of plant selections and propagating methods.

I never bore of being witness to the amazement on a child's face when they first see the signs of leaves from a seed that they had planted. These experiences however small they may seem to an adult, can be a life changing exercise for children of all ages and even adults can get a jolt of satisfaction and a good dose of 'look what I did' from a successful propagating experience. Taking the time to teach children about plants, the environment and gardens is an investment for life.

GROWING FROM SEED: THE RECIPE
Ingredients
- Choose easy to germinate varieties and make sure it is the right season for that particular vegetable or flower.
- Seed raising mix preferably certified organic
- Container to germinate seeds in or prepared garden bed

SEED CHOICE:

My pick of easy winners for spring sowing success are radish, zucchini, squash, corn, sunflowers, nasturtiums, beans, snow peas, tomatoes, cucumbers and pumpkins.

Of course you do not have to stick to my recommendations and choice of seed will depend on what's in season in your particular location.

- A great idea is to choose heirloom varieties of these and explain to your child/children the importance of preserving these old fashioned and rare types of flowers and vegetables. Another bonus with heirloom varieties is that they set seed true to type, meaning that you can successfully save seed from these plants knowing that it will grow exactly the same as the parent plant, unlike hybrid varieties. Obviously organic, GM free selections are advised as some non-organic seeds can be dusted in nasty chemicals.
- Seed raising mixes ready to go can be easily bought from most hardware, produce and garden centres. There are usually organic options.
- Containers: This is where it can be great to discuss the importance of recycling. Use old cut up egg cartons, toilet rolls and newspaper to create your very own jiffy pots. Old yoghurt containers can be good too, as long as you make sure you put drainage holes in the bottom.

- Even easier is to sow your seed directly into a prepared garden bed.

Note: smaller seeds are often best started off in containers. If you wish sow finer seeds directly into the garden make sure you prepare your soil to a fine tilth, so that the little seeds can germinate and set down roots easily.

Method 1: Container /indirect sowing

1. Get your little gardener to fill their container of choice to the top with seed raising mix and lightly tap down.
2. Take your seed of choice and carefully follow the instructions on how deep the seed should be planted. This will vary depending on seed type and variety. General rule of thumb is two to three times the diameter of the seed.
3. Then water carefully with a fine mist liquid seaweed fertiliser. Mix as per instructions given on bottle. Water alone is fine; seaweed just gets them off to a good start.
4. Then water little and often, keeping the mix moist but not wet.
5. Once the adult leaves appear (the 2nd set of leaves), it is time to either plant your little green babies into the garden or pot them on into a larger container using a potting mix.
6. Remember to label your containers with the type of seed planted and the date

Method 2: Garden beds/direct sowing

1. Prepare soil to a fine tilth. A fine tilth is where the soil is sifted and graded until it has no lumps or solid objects in it. This can be achieved by raking over the soil and breaking up any large lumps of soil, removing any debris and then raking until you have a smooth flat soil surface. The addition of well-rotted compost during this exercise would be beneficial.
2. Now dig furrows within your garden bed
3. Plant your seed of choice. Again a general rule of thumb when planting seeds is to plant them at a depth of two to three times the seeds diameter. It is better to sow too shallow than too deep. Follow seed packet directions on spacing requirements.
4. Now adhering to the advice above, cover your seeds with the correct amount of soil, remembering not to have them sown too deeply and pat down soil firmly.
5. Water gently with a seaweed liquid fertiliser solution.
6. Once again mark/label where your seeds have been sown, what they are and when they were planted. Old iceblock sticks make great seedling name markers.

** *Germination: this will depend on the type of seed chosen, some plants like radish can germinate in a couple of days where as onions can take up to three weeks or more.*

OTHER FUNTASTIC PROJECTS:

Sprout World

This would have to one of the easiest and quickest way to germinate seeds. All you need is some cotton wool, a container, sprouting seeds of choice and water. A successful harvest can still be achieved even if you have no garden.

Jar lids, half eggshells and eggcups all make cheap and easy containers to grow your sprouts in. There of course are many sprouting devices available. Some are multi layer growing towers for the mad keen 'sprouter' and there are some easy-use jars as well.

All you need to do is keep the seeds continually moist and in a brightly lit position while germinating and growing. Harvest when first or second leaves appear.

What seeds can you use? Radish, sunflower, cress, mustard, fenugreek, alfalfa, mung beans and snowpeas.

Marvellous Micro Greens

These are becoming extremely popular around the globe, you can even buy complete micro green kits and books on the topic.

Micro greens tend to be varieties of leafy vegetables such lettuce mixes, Asian greens, broccoli, beetroot, rocket, chervil, kale, endive and sprouting seed choices can also be used. These are just grown for their juvenile foliage and heaps of fun can be had snipping the tops off, to add to salads, sandwiches and the dinner plate as an edible garnish, a bit like sprouts.

Your micro green crop can be grown in the same way as you would if just doing general sprouting but you can also grow them in seedling trays, pots, really whatever container takes your fancy, just add seed raising mix, water and light.

Claire Bickle is a qualified Brisbane based horticulturalist, having a Diploma in Horticulture and an Advanced Design Certificate in Permaculture Design

YOGA for KIDS

Creating Family Yoga Sanctuaries at Home
by *Kylie De Giorgio*

Having a yoga sanctuary in your home creates a special haven for your family. It encourages them to stretch and strengthen their bodies, relax and quite their minds, bringing reduced stress and increased well-being. Everyone is more likely to practice yoga at home if there is a special, inviting space created just for it.

You can use a corner in the kids' and parent's bedrooms or in any room you like. Set up the space with your child with enthusiasm and as a gift of peace and relaxation for all of you. Keep the space comfortable, clean and free of clutter.

Decorate the parent's yoga space with pictures of spiritual role models that inspire. Images of Aum (the primordial sound of the universe), fresh flowers and a meditation candle (lit when practicing yoga) make the space sacred.

Create the kids' space with pictures of children practicing calming poses, and decorate it together to make it sacred to your child in their own way.

Some ideas are:
- love crystal (rose quartz)
- special yoga bells
- fresh flowers hand picked together
- yoga mandala or yantra
- beautiful blanket chosen for relaxation
- eye pillow made for your child, filled with lavender and linseeds
- calming aromatherapy (safely placed).

Children will often want you to share in their yoga playfulness. When they do, grab a mat and practice alongside them in the spirit of fun and connectedness.

The yoga sequence:

Siddhasana - Seated Meditation Pose:

Sitting with one ankle in front of the other, lift spine. Close eyes. Let go of distracting thoughts by focusing on your breath. Dedicate yourself to peace and harmony.

Chant Aum three times.

Adho Mukha Svanasana - Downward Facing Dog:

In all fours position, lift knees off ground and straighten back, legs and arms to come into pose. Move shoulders away from ears.

Relax neck and look towards knees. Lift buttocks towards the ceiling.

Trikonasana - The Triangle Pose:

Little ones like to come into this pose singing I'm a Little Teapot, tipping over and pouring themselves out into the full pose. Place feet one leg length apart on mat. Turn left foot in towards right and right foot to 90 degrees. Arms at shoulder height at sides. On exhale, pivot from hips to extend out and over right side as shown. Breathe.

Release and repeat on other side.

Bhujangasana - Cobra Snake Pose:

Lying on belly, hands under shoulders slowly lift head, shoulders and chest off floor on in-breath. Relax shoulders away from ears.

Exhale and release. Play in the pose as rattle snakes, big mummy, daddy and small baby snakes, and even cobras dancing to a snake charmer's flute.

Bharadjvasana - Seated Twist Pose:

Sitting, swing bent legs to the left as shown. Place left ankle in inner arch of right foot. Lift spine, place left hand on right knee, right hand behind you. Breathe in through nose, twist from hips to right. Breathe and hold position.

Release and repeat on other side.

Half Paschimottanasana - Seated Forward Bend:

Sit with legs bent, lift spine. Play one potato, two potato, three potato, four with hands, elbows resting on knees.

When finished, rest forehead on closed 'potato' fists with eyes closed for a few moments.

Savasana - Relaxation Pose:

Lie down and rest with eye pillow over eyes. Play quiet, gentle background music. Lead your child on a relaxing journey through the body as they breathe in qualities of love, then peace, then happiness into every cell of their body. Do the same for yourself.

Relax, release and let go.

To end your practice, sit for a moment in silence with your family to honour the practice of yoga, and give thanks to everyone who practiced with you.

Namaste

Kylie De Giorgio is the director of Simply Kids Yoga and also provides professional, specialised kids yoga teacher training to qualified yoga teachers.

YOGA SETS YOU UP FOR LIFE

Kids Yoga Classes
Mums & Bubs and Tots Yoga
Private Family Yoga
Yoga Workshops and Birthday Parties

Yoga helps kids gain strong, balanced and flexible bodies,
clear and creative minds and gain access to their spiritual selves.
Connect mind, body and breath for peace and relaxation for the whole family.
May your days be filled with love, wonder, childhood laughter and yoga relaxations.

For more information call Kylie De Giorgio on 0416 162 755, or visit www.kidsyoga.com.au

SIMPLY KIDS YOGA

BOOK REVIEWS

by Sharon Dowley

Children's Books

On My Way to a Happy Life
Author: Deepak Chopra
Illustrator: Rosemary Woods
Hay House Australia
$19.95

Deepak Chopra is one of the west's leading exponents of Eastern philosophy. He's a physician, founder of The Chopra Centre for Wellbeing in California, and with over 6 0 books to his name that have been translated into 35 languages, there's no doubt he is something of a force in the publishing arena.

Chopra's focus is on alternative medicine, the mind-body connection and the 'spiritual laws' of the universe. In response to feedback from readers that they wished they had learnt his spiritual laws at a younger age, Chopra last year published On My Way to a Happy Life, his latest book for children.

On My Way to a Happy Life is designed to introduce young children to Chopra's teachings in a simple and fun way. The principles are beliefs that any parent might wish for their child: anything is possible, giving and getting, acceptance, growing what you want, being open to new ways and ideas. Reading his words in the pages of a children's book, it seems almost the perfect vehicle for his teachings. Simply put, this is a sweet book with a positive message: success and happiness is based not on what you do or what you acquire, but on who you are.

Illustrator Rosemary Woods has filled each page with tiny figures and animals, gardens and flowers, mountains and waterfalls, stars and planets. Envisage dancing tigers, elephants on rocket ships and flying pigs. In short, it's a cornucopia of lively and colourful images for children to explore and it's yet another enticing element of this charming book.

A Forest
IMarc Martin
Penguin Books
$24.95

It begins with a classic fairy tale flourish, "There once was a forest". Yet those anticipating princes, princesses, heroes or heroines will find something quite different. In fact, the only 'characters' in Marc Martin's debut children's story, A Forest, are the forest itself, and a city. Like many a popular adventure however, there is a duel - and a victor. A Forest is a very simple tale of rebirth and renewal, and it's an opportunity for young children to see, in a very simple fashion, the consequences of exploiting our natural world.

Marc Martin is an illustrator and graphic designer based in Melbourne. He uses a combination of watercolour, textas, ink, pencil and computer and the result are drawings that are quirky, sweet and somewhat reminiscent of classic vintage illustrations. Given his background, the emphasis on graphics over words is not surprising. Yet while the story itself couldn't be simpler, it's also surprisingly touching, and it does resonate. This tale of nature abused and reborn will provide parents with an ideal springboard with which to teach children about the value of nature and the consequences of uncontrolled urban development. It will also hopefully inspire in children an interest in the natural world.

Martin apparently self-published an edition of this in 2008, but this gorgeous version has been given the professional publisher's treatment. If you enjoy it, pay a visit to his website (www.marcmartin.com.au) where you'll also find a range of posters and prints featuring his decorative style that would look a treat in any child's bedroom.

Adult Books

A Modern Woman's Guide to A Natural Empowering Birth
Katrina Zaslavsky
$34.95

As the title makes clear, this release from author and natural health advocate, Katrina Zaslavsky is designed as a guide to a positive, natural and ultimately empowering birth experience. It's essentially a collection of natural birth stories, and tips from professionals including midwives, doulas, fertility specialists and GP's. Its focus is to encourage women to embrace the magic of birth, overcome fears and prepare both body, and mind, for the birth experience.

Zaslavsky has worked in the natural health arena for many years, is a columnist for Holistic Bliss Magazine and the author of a popular monthly online publication, Empower Yourself. She says the idea for this book came about from her own search whilst pregnant, for a birth guide that wasn't clinical or negative. In creating this book, she interviewed a range of mums and those working in the health field.

The book is divided into 'insights', along the lines of 'knowledge is birth power', 'harness your hormones' and 'trust your instincts'. And each is comprised of personal stories and

quotes. There' also an afterword by Dr Sarah Buckley MD, author of Gentle Birth, Gentle Mothering.

Zaslavsky's passion for natural birth and natural living is obvious. The ultimate magic of birth is of course the gorgeous little creature that comes into the world, regardless of whether it's been a natural or problematic birth. For any expectant mum however, this is a positive and inspiring addition to the pregnancy bookshelf.

 We asked our Facebook community which parenting book was their favourite. The most favourite parenting book was *Heart to Heart Parenting* by Robin Grille. Other were:

- *Buddhism for Mothers* by Sarah Napthali (Emma & Serene)
- *Unconditional Parenting* by Alfie Kohn (Catherine & Alicia)
- *The happiest Toddler in the Block* by Harvey Karp (Peggy & Melissa)
- *The Wonder Weeks* by Dr Frans Plooj & Dr Hetty van de Rijt (Lauren & Ally)
- *Helping your baby to sleep- why gentle techniques work best* by Anni Gethin & Beth Macgregor (Karly)
- *The No-Cry Sleep Solution* by Elizabeth Pantley (Kate)
- *Raising Boys* by Steve Biddulf (Debbie & Isabella)
- *Baby Love* by Robin Barker (Kate)
- *Kids Are Worth It* by Barbara Coloroso (Kathryn)
- *Well Adjusted Babies* by Dr Jennifer Barham-Floreani (April)
- *Raising Our Children Raising Ourselves* by Naomi Aldort (Alicia)

Go to www.facebook.com/NurtureParentingMagazine to read all the bits and pieces!

EDITORS PICK

Helping your Baby to Sleep: Why Gentle Techniques Work Best
Anni Gethin & Beth Macgregor
Finch Publishing
$29.95

For many new parents, sleep – or lack of – may become an all too consuming issue. A common misconception is that it's 'normal' for bubs to sleep through the night at a young age, yet the reality for a large percentage is certainly quite different. Prolonged night waking can be very difficult for both bubs and parents, with fatigue spurring parents to try various techniques to help babies sleep through the night.

Australian health specialists, Anni Gethin and Beth Macgregor (Gethin is a health social scientist and Macgregor a psychologist) have cast their eye over the sleep issue in yet another book dedicated to the subject. This is not essentially a sleep guide however. Instead it examines 'sleep training' or 'control crying', arguing that babies are ill-prepared to cope with this much-advocated sleep method, that it interferes with the natural bonding process, and that there may be long-term negative effects.

The first section of the books looks at why babies wake through the night, and uses scientific studies to argue that babies need to be comforted at all costs. In the second section, the authors suggest gentle methods to help parents help bubs to sleep.

The first section in particular provides thoughtful reading. Although the authors do acknowledge that a little crying is normal, a relief no doubt for parents who at times have not responded to babies immediately through sheer exhaustion, I was genuinely curious about how much the authors believe is too much.

Originally published in 2007, and with an updated edition released last year, this book aims to help parents feel more confident about parenting and it's certainly a worthwhile and thought-provoking read for any new parent or parent-to-be.

Product Reviews:

Kala's Magic No Spill Cup ~300ml
by Kala
$14.95

We had a rule in our family 'No food or Drinks in the car' ~ well that has now changed to just 'No Food'! This cup is magic ~ the spout features a fabulous one way valve to ensure no spills. It allows babies / children to easily drink (no strong suction required), and has large handles on both sides for easy grip. It holds 300ml and comes in three colours (purple, blue and green)

It is also very durable as it has been dropped many times and nothing has broken!

From conscious point of view, it is 100% Australian made and is BPA free.

Check out
www.mummyslittlehelper.com.au

There are so many options when it comes to buying clothes. However, quality is always at the top of my priorities. That is why I was so impressed with this top and headband from Growing Footprints. The quality is second to none. It is beautifully stitched and the material is quite thick. Also, the cotton is 100% organic, so there are no nasties hiding in the fabric.

The design is also to die for. It has cuteness and elegance all in one. It would suit any little princess (sorry about the gender stereotype!)

Available at
www.growingfootprints.com.au

Marshmallow Top
by Growing footprints
$25.95

Organic Cotton Deluxe Baby Wipes
by Nature's Child
$24.95

Have you ever wondered if there was an environmentally sustainable alternative to disposable nappy wipes? Well, here it is! Reusable organic cotton nappy wipes. They have supersoft brushed flanelette cotton on one side and absorbent terry towelling on the other side. There are three in the pack and each is 18 x 30cm.

I keep a small tub of water near the changetable with a clothe in it. At the end of each day, I change the water and put the wipe in the wash. They can also be used in the bath as a supersoft wash cloth! There is also the monetary advantage of not continually buying nappy wipes!

Available at
www.natureschild.com.au

Baby clothes can be bought anywhere. But clothing that is organic, practical, and looks great is hard to find. Well, look no further! This striped pring onsie by Tiny Twig fits all of that criteria. It is lightweight, soft and comes in a range of colours.

Not only does their clothing look great, they are also conscious manufactures as they use organically cultivated cotton, which is purchased from the small farmers through fair trade means.

Available at
www.tinytwig.com.au

Striped Jumpsuit
by Tiny Twig
$29.95

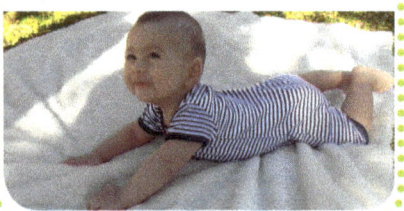

Baby Bath & Body Wash
by Brauer
$11.49

Brauer have just released their new line of baby products. As you can expect from a company committed to natural ingredients, their baby products are free from pertrochemicals.

The Baby Bath and Body Wash is packed full of natural ingredients, including paw paw, shea butter, honey & carrot oil. It also feels lovely on the skin and has a lovely aroma.

Each of Brauer's products in its baby range comes with a little bath duckie which will also provide hours of amusement for your little one in the bath!

Check out www.brauer.com.au

Lil Puddins have the formula right. The nappy is made from bamboo fibre, so is soft, flexible and very absorbant. It has seven layers of bamboo- one for the pocket, a triple liner and a triple booster. It also has multiple snaps to fit various sizes so the one nappy can be used for a baby and small child.

Further, Lil Puddins use an IMO Certified and Global Organic Textile Standard (GOTS) approved manufacturer. They also use an environmentally friendly fabric exportation company!

Available at
www.lilpuddins.com.au

Bamboo Modern Cloth Nappy
by Lil Puddins
$30.00

Featured Reviews: Secret Women's Business!

Ju Ju Cup
by Ju Ju
$63.00

The Ju Ju cup is is a reusable menstrual cup made from medical-grade silicone - it is used instead of tampons or pads. It is inserted like a tampon, but unlike tampons, there are no chemicals or toxins.

At first I was a little skeptical - not sure whether I would like it, but three cycles on, I am converted. Every 12 hours I empty it (into a toilet), rinse it off with water and reinsert for another 12 hours. In addition to being environmentally friendly (nothing is thrown away), it is also cost efficient as one cup can last between 5 to 10 years.

I found though that the best thing about the Ju Ju Cup is that there is no smell (you know what I mean) as it is all kept internal.

Check out www.jujucup.com.au

The first remedy most people will think of when you have sore or cracked nipples is cream or nipple shields (usually made from plastic). However there is now a natural alternative to shield, protect and help heal your nipples.

The Shells shield your nipple from rubbing on your bra easing any sensitivity or pain you may have. For cracked nipples the Shells ease pain quickly and by using your own breast milk in conjunction with the Shells, cracks and wounds heal quickly

The best part is that they are a natural shape so you can wear the Shells when you go out and no one will know you have them on (and you don't get that sticky feeling that you do with the creams!).

Visit www.petitebisou.com.au

Bebe-Nacre Breast Shells
by Bebe-Nacre
$49.95

If you are a little embarrassed about breastfeeding in public you probably have been scouring the internet trying to find nice, affordable nursing tops. Well, look no further! Moome Nursingwear specialise in affordable and practical nursing tops.

This top looks great for the pending summer days and has a cleverly designed opening that allows your baby to latch on without you needing to show any skin. It is made from 95% cotton 5% spandex, so it is light and airy.

Moome also have many other designs that can complete in your spring and summer wardrobe!

**Check out
www.moomenursingwear.com**

Breastfeeding Top
by Moome Nursingwear
$25.00

Reusable Cotton Pads
by Rad Pads
$22.50

When I first heard about resusable cotton pads I screwed my face up. Then I thought about all the chemicals and artificial fragrances that go into them, and consequently on me.

So I tried the cotton pads. Each of the pads consists of the outer case including the wings, plus the appropriate sized toweling insert e.g. small, medium, large or extra large insert. It certainly felt nicer on my skin than the disposible pads.

My initial reaction to washing it was again to screw my face up. But after a couple of times, it was nothing

Available at www.rad-pads.com

f alittlebird.com.au
🐦 alittlebirdkids

What's on?   Where to go?   What do to?

A Little Bird told me; don't get into a flap, we have a nest full of ideas and information for families.

www.alittlebird.com.au is a one-stop online resource full of ideas, activities and things to do for kids and babies. Come fly with us as we build a community of happy, healthy parents and kids via our easy-to-use website and popular Facebook Page.

National Events for Kids & Bubs

A Little Bird told us about some inspiring days out for parents and some fun days to share with your kids. All around Australia, there's loads of things happening to keep the little ones entertained.

National Children's Week
20th - 28th October
"A Caring World Shares": celebrating children's right to enjoy childhood This week is also a time for children to demonstrate their talents, skills and abilities in one of the many activities near you.
www.childrensweek.org.au

National Nutritional Week
14th - 20th October
Helping you to make healthy choices for you and your family. Nutrition week also includes World Food Day and Nude Food Day.
www.nutritionaustralia.org/national/event/2012/national-nutrition-week

The First National Health and PE Day
5th September
Promoting healthy fun in schools and in the wider community for children and young people.
www.achper.org.au/news/national-health-pe-day

National Recycling Week
12th - 17th November
Planet Ark's National Recycling Week campaign promotes the importance of reducing, reusing and recycling! It's great to be green!
www.recyclingweek.planetark.org/

Save the Koala Month
All throughout September
With less than 20% of Koala's habitat remaining it's time to build awareness and help fundraise.
https://www.savethekoala.com/

Father's Day
2nd September
Happy Father's Day to all the dads! Find something to do with Dad on his special day on A Little Bird.
www.alittlebird.com.au

What's On...

QUEENSLAND

Playgroup Dress Up Day
21st September
Dress up just a little or in a crazy way to help support very young children.
www.playgroupqld.com.au

Nurture's Babywearing Event
12th October 10am
Head down to New Farm park for some babywearing activities and giveaways with the team at Nurture.
www.nurtureparentingmagazine.com.au

NEW SOUTH WALES

Glebe Street Fair 2012
18th November
From 9am enjoy scrumptious food, crafts for kiddies and adults, dedicated kid's activities and more!
www.glebestreetfair.com

Biennal Family Sunday
2nd September
Special family days at Cockatoo Island all about having fun together, creating, looking and engaging.
www.bos18.com

VICTORIA

September Festival
22nd - 23rd September
The fun-filled festival will be full of dancing, shows and fireworks; fun for the whole family.
www.septemberfestival.com.au

Connecting with Families: through community, culture and collaboration
15th - 16th November
Come along and find out how families can be supported by multi-disciplinary professional in today's culture.
www.aifs.govspace.gov.au

TASMANIA

Hobart Christmas Pageant
18th November
Come and see Santa Claus in this wonderfully traditional Christmas street parade.
www.hobartcity.com.au

Royal Hobart Show
24th - 27th October
You've gotta go to the Royal Hobart Show! There's so much entertainment on offer and fantastic show jumping to see.
www.hobartshowground.com.au

NORTHERN TERRITORY

Palmerston Festival
31st August - 1st September
The festival begins with a fabulous Friday night market and goes on to a family fun day on Saturday.
www.palmerston.nt.gov.au/city/about-palmerston/palmerston-festival

Christmas in Palmerston
25th November
Come and celebrate the start of the Christmas season with your whole family and sing along with the carols.
www.travelnt.com

SOUTH AUSTRALIA

Baby and Kids Market
18th November
The biggest, and best, baby and kids market out there; come and grab some beautiful bargains.
www.babykidsmarket.com.au

Port Broughton Annual Rubber Duck Race
30th September
Come and race the rubber ducks or take part in the Yellow Duck Hunt or the Duck and Spoon Race! Good ole fashioned fun!
www.southaustralia.com

WESTERN AUSTRALIA

Fremantle Festival
4th November
The Childrens Fiesta at Samson Park will be full of colour, music and celebrations. Not to be missed!
www.fremantle.wa.gov.au/festivals/Fremantle_Festival

Directory

Nurture
Australia's Natural Parenting Magazine

Physical • Emotional • Intellectual • Spiritual

Australia's natural parenting magazine for conscious parents

Including articles on: breastfeeding, birthing, organic gardening, parent/child activities, baby-led weaning recipes, eco travel & more!

Subscribe online now: www.nurtureparentingmagazine.com.au   www.facebook.com/NurtureParentingMagazine

---

Yes, I would like to subscribe to **Nurture**!

Please choose:
- ☐ 1 yr subscription (4 issues) $31.80 AUD
- ☐ 2 yr subscription (8 issues) $63.60 AUD
- ☐ 1 yr Online subscription (4 issues) $19.95 AUD

Name: _____

Postal address: _____

_____

_____

Email: _____

Phone: _____

online subscriptions now available

Credit card payment:

☐ Visa   ☐ Mastercard

Name on card: _____

Credit card number: ☐☐☐☐ ☐☐☐☐ ☐☐☐☐ ☐☐☐☐   Card expiry date: _____

I authorise the following amount to be debited from my credit card: $ _____

Please mail your completed subscription form to
2 Flora Court Cornubia, Queensland 4130

Thank you for your subscription. We hope you enjoy 'Nurture', Australia's Natural Parenting Magazine.

www.ingramcontent.com/pod-product-compliance
Lightning Source LLC
Chambersburg PA
CBHW061538010526
44107CB00067B/2901